AF326700

How to Stop Being Negative, Rude, and Hurtful 5-in-1

The Complete Guide to Boost Positivity, Calm Anger, Speak with Kindness, Practice Gratitude, and Spread Respect

VIVIAN WHITMORE

Claim Your Free Bonus

As a thank you for reading, I've put together a powerful digital bonus pack to help you apply what you've learned — even if you only have a few minutes a day.

 **Inside you'll find:**

✔ Quick-access emotional reset tools
✔ A printable clarity map for focus and purpose
✔ 30 powerful journaling prompts
✔ Daily progress & reflection trackers
✔ A mini affirmation deck for calm and confidence

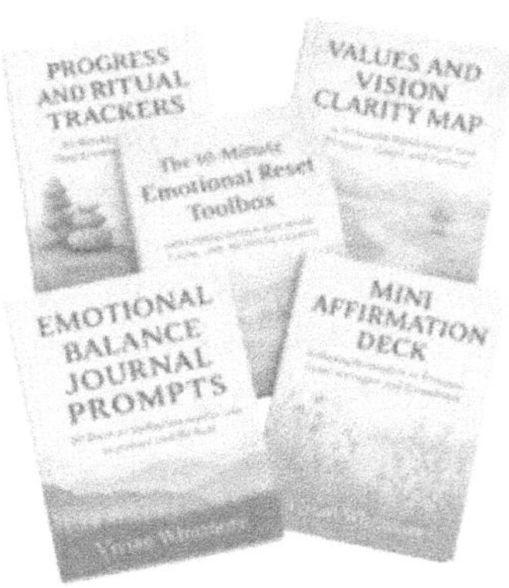

Access below to download your full bonus pack:

https://livetolearn.lpages.co/vivian-withmore-how-to-stop-being-negative-rude-and-hurtful-5-in-1-paperback/

Or, scan the QR code

<u>**REVIEW ON:**</u>

How to Stop Being Negative, Rude and Hurtful 5-in-1: The Complete Guide to Boost Productivity, Calm Anger, Speak with Kindness, Practice Gratitude, and Spread Respect

By: Carolina Estevez, Psy.D., Licensed Psychologist

How to Stop Being Negative, Rude and Hurtful 5-in-1: The Complete Guide to Boost Productivity, Calm Anger, Speak with Kindness, Practice Gratitude, and Spread Respect is an excellent multi-volume collection offering a thoughtful, well-structured, and clinically informed roadmap for personal growth, emotional regulation, and healthier interpersonal functioning. As a psychologist, I appreciate the author's clear integration of evidence-based techniques across cognitive-behavioral therapy, mindfulness, interpersonal effectiveness skills, and positive psychology. The five-book structure allows readers to explore change through multiple dimensions—thought patterns, emotional regulation, communication, gratitude, and respect— each reinforcing the others in meaningful ways.

Book 1, which focuses on rewiring negative thinking patterns, provides an accessible introduction to cognitive distortions, behavioral experiments, and attentional training. The incorporation of the HEAL method and emphasis on building agency align with current neuroscience findings on neuroplasticity and emotional learning. This section is an excellent resource for readers seeking practical steps to interrupt habitual negativity and establish healthier mental habits.

Anger regulation with a clinically grounded understanding of anger as both a biological response and an informational signal is discussed in Book 2. The chapters on breathwork, rumination interruption, problem-solving, and HRV tracking reflect modern approaches to physiological and psychological regulation. I found the discussion of hostile attribution bias particularly valuable; it is a common yet often overlooked contributor to chronic anger. The book's focus on reshaping the internal narrative around anger will resonate with many individuals seeking more adaptive coping strategies.

Book 3 shifts toward interpersonal communication, offering practical and research-supported techniques for speaking with clarity and compassion. The inclusion of Nonviolent Communication, assertiveness training through the DESC script, empathy development, and conflict repair provides a comprehensive interpersonal toolkit. This section is especially useful for individuals seeking to improve relationship satisfaction, as it captures both the mechanics of communication and the emotional attunement necessary for meaningful connection.

Gratitude, not as a superficial exercise, but as a clinically significant intervention with measurable benefits on stress, mood, and overall well-being is covered in Book 4. The emphasis on journaling, relational appreciation, and resilience-building is consistent with the positive psychology literature and offers readers structured ways to deepen their sense of meaning.

Finally, Book 5 offers a strong exploration of boundaries, fairness, respect, and values-based living. This book stands out for its clarity in explaining the reciprocal nature of respect and the psychological importance of healthy limits. The boundary scripts and reflections on integrity provide readers with actionable guidance for building healthier relationships rooted in mutual regard.

Overall, this collection is insightful, practical, and grounded in psychological science. It provides a holistic framework that readers can apply immediately while also fostering deeper self- awareness and long-term emotional growth.

TABLE OF CONTENTS

INTRODUCTION
LAYING THE FOUNDATION FOR TRANSFORMATION

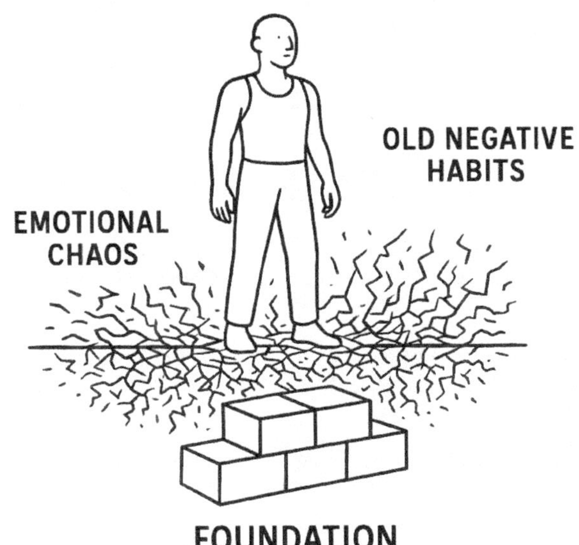

Let's be honest. You are here because the way you react to the world, the things you say, or the thoughts you carry are hurting you. You might feel a constant knot of tension in your shoulders. Maybe you carry a low hum of worry every day. Perhaps you snap at the people you love most, only to regret the words immediately after. That cycle is exhausting. It keeps you isolated and prevents you from living the genuinely connected life you want.

You might believe that negativity, short-fused anger, or habitual rudeness are simply character traits. They are not. They are deeply ingrained habits. They are predictable behavioral patterns rooted in your psychology and biology.

This guide provides a systematic, evidence-based plan to dismantle those patterns. We are not aiming for fake, forced optimism. We are working toward genuine, measurable, and lasting change. This is the complete operating manual for rebuilding your emotional life.

The Hidden Cost of Living Hostile

The way we talk to ourselves and others carries a high price tag. Chronic negativity and a habit of hostility actively diminish your quality of life. They create a wall between you and healthy social connections. When people engage in hostile habits, they often experience isolation and persistent psychological distress.

But the cost extends far beyond feeling bad. Research confirms that constantly suppressing or exhibiting chronic anger affects your physical health. People who habitually restrain or display intense anger face significant measurable risks. These risks include reduced social support, lower relationship quality, and a heightened susceptibility to conditions like chronic pain and coronary heart disease. Your hostility is not just a social friction point. It is a serious physiological issue that demands structured intervention.

The problem is often rooted in inflexible thinking. These are thought patterns that just don't bend, leading you to misinterpret others or catastrophize minor setbacks. These rigid habits become fuel for self-criticism and destructive behaviors. It is crucial to recognize this truth: the problem is a functional impairment, not a moral failure. The path forward involves both adjusting the mental software and improving the physical integrity of your brain's regulatory system.

The Science of Why You Feel Stuck

To fix these habits, we must first look at your brain. Our brains are not built for constant modern happiness. They are built for ancient survival. This means the brain has an inherent tendency toward caution and threat detection. It is called the negativity bias.

This bias means your brain is specifically wired to notice, learn from, and use negative information much more readily than positive information. This is an affective asymmetry. It served an important function long ago, helping your ancestors avoid danger. But today, this neurobiological default often fosters anxiety, perseverative thought, and depressive behaviors. Because of this hardwired tendency, developing a genuinely positive outlook requires conscious, structured effort. You must deliberately work to reverse this natural, ancient wiring.

Chronic stress and long periods of negativity compound this problem. This chronic state leads to negative neuroplasticity. We can actually observe this as a weakening of beneficial neural connections. It includes synaptic loss and neuronal atrophy within key regions like the medial prefrontal cortex (mPFC) and the hippocampus. The prefrontal cortex (PFC) is the key structure for regulating emotions. When these structures are damaged by chronic stress, your ability to regulate feelings becomes functionally impaired. You literally lose control over your impulses and moods.

Changing long-standing negative habits, therefore, requires two actions: adjusting your thought patterns through cognitive restructuring, and repairing the underlying neural structures through positive neuroplasticity.

A major reason you feel stuck is a psychological state known as learned helplessness.This is a conditioned loss of effort. It happens when you feel you have no control over repetitive stressors or failures, leading to deep hopelessness. Chemically, this feeling corresponds to a dampening of striatal dopamine synthesis.

Dopamine is the primary neurotransmitter for motivation and reward. When motivation diminishes, you experience burnout and inertia. Chronic exposure to psychosocial stress causes this dopamine dampening, effectively putting your brain's reward circuits offline.It is not a failure of willpower. It is a reversible brain state.

The Scientific Case for Immediate Action

The great promise of modern neuroscience is neuroplasticity. Your brain changes constantly based on your experiences and your mental habits. This means you have the power to actively overwrite negative emotional programming. This is why both pharmacological treatments and psychotherapies like Cognitive Behavioral Therapy (CBT) work.

They decrease the hyperactivity of the limbic structures, the parts that scream "danger", while increasing the regulatory power of the cortical structures, the parts that say, "Stop and think".

The immediate solution to feeling stuck is conscious behavioral action. When you perceive that your action produces a result, dopamine levels rise almost instantly. This rise restores the brain's reward circuit and affirms your belief in personal agency. This feeling of agency can return quickly. This foundational principle is the core of Action-Oriented Therapy: using concrete, purposeful actions to improve your well-being and overcome challenges. This entire guide is built on this principle. We use practical action to systematically restore motivation, confidence, and self-worth.

This comprehensive guide organizes your transformation into five interconnected, action-oriented systems. We start with internal repair and move toward effective, respectful external interaction. This sequence builds a solid psychological and neurological foundation for all future changes.

Book 1: Rewire Your Brain: Action Steps to Boost Positivity

The first book is about internal reconstruction. It focuses on dismantling negative self-talk and actively building new, positive neural pathways. We use the tested tools of CBT to target internal thoughts and beliefs. The goal is to identify and test the common cognitive errors: the irrational ways your mind twists reality. We move from fixed despair to objective, testable data. We then use Rick Hanson's HEAL method to systematically "take in the good," enriching positive experiences to promote joy, confidence, and inner peace. This practice creates measurable increases in happiness and self-compassion.

Book 2: Take Back Control: Techniques to Calm Anger Now

The second book focuses on immediate, physiological intervention. Before you can change an angry thought, you must calm the angry body. We restore calm using science-based bodily techniques that directly reduce physiological arousal. The 4-7-8 breathing protocol is a prime example.

This technique actively stimulates the respiratory vagus nerve, which counteracts the fight-or-flight stress response. We will teach you how to measure your calm using Heart Rate Variability (HRV), a physiological index of how well your body regulates itself. This book shifts anger management from a subjective feeling to an objective, self-monitored skill. It trains you to interrupt damaging rumination and replace the hostile attribution bias with rational thought .

Book 3: Connect Clearly: Actionable Models for Kind Speech

The third book addresses your external interactions. The aim is to replace damaging, judgmental language with clear, assertive, and empathetic dialogue. Rudeness is often miscommunication, where your intent is lost in your delivery. We introduce the foundational framework of Nonviolent Communication (NVC). NVC trains you to express your observations, feelings, and underlying universal human needs without resorting to judgment or blame.

This approach builds connection rather than conflict. We also introduce the DESC script for structured assertiveness, helping you ask for what you want directly and honestly while respecting the rights of others. Assertiveness reduces stress and boosts self-esteem.

Book 4: Build Inner Strength: Daily Habits for Practicing Gratitude

The fourth book focuses on deepening your emotional resilience. Gratitude is not just being polite. It is a specific, evidence-based psychological intervention. It serves as a therapeutic tool for addressing symptoms of anxiety and depression. Meta-analysis shows gratitude interventions lead to measurable improvements in mental health and positive mood. We explore how gratitude practices physiologically counter core stress hormones.

The practice reduces cortisol levels, which helps detoxify your stress system. It builds lasting internal resources by leveraging the clinical benefits of gratitude, including better sleep and increased resilience during hard times. We show you how structured journaling and appreciation letters build durable neural changes in the brain's social pathways.

Book 5: Define Your Space: Practical Actions to Spread Respect

The final book focuses on self-worth, boundary setting, and maintaining balanced, healthy social relationships. Respect is fundamentally about reciprocity. Social Exchange Theory confirms that relationships thrive when rewards outweigh costs and balance is maintained. This book helps you define your value and spread respect by demanding and giving fair regard.

We define boundaries as essential self-care practices that protect your mental health and prevent burnout . Using the communication tools from Book 3, you learn to set clear limits with conviction and care, ensuring your needs are met. This book provides the practical actions necessary to live your core values, which is the highest form of self-respect.

How to Use This Action Guide

This guide provides clinically validated methods in an accessible, direct format. The structure moves you from recognizing internal distortions to setting necessary relational limits. The efficacy of these methods relies entirely on consistent, deliberate practice.

Treat each book as a laboratory. You will test assumptions about your thoughts and behaviors. You must be willing to engage in the specific actions: writing in your journal, practicing the breathing techniques, and scripting difficult conversations. The sustained effort of applying these tools will physically shape your brain and redefine your interactions with the world.

Change begins with belief in agency. This guide proves that your actions matter, and they will produce results.

Deepening the Scientific Foundation: The Mind-Body Connection in Change

The success of this five-part system relies on fully understanding the continuous feedback loop between your mind and your body. Negative emotions are not confined to subjective experience. They are chemical and physiological states that require physiological intervention.

Emotional regulation depends on a continuous balance. This balance exists between the reasoning power of the prefrontal cortex (PFC) and the rapid, fear-based responses of the limbic system, specifically the amygdala.

When you are chronically stressed or angry, the limbic system is hyperactive. It overrides your PFC's ability to think clearly or rationally. This is why trying to be rational when you are furious just does not work. Your ancient brain takes over, prioritizing impulse over reasoned response.

This explains why the techniques in *Calm Anger* are foundational. The breathing exercises provide a direct, non-cognitive pathway to downregulate the stress response. By engaging the respiratory vagus nerve, you force your body out of sympathetic activation, the fight-or-flight state, and into parasympathetic activation, the rest-and-digest state. This physical calm is the necessary precondition that restores PFC function.

When you slow your heart rate and increase your heart rate variability (HRV), your body signals to your brain that the immediate threat is over. This physical peace creates the neural space required for the cognitive work in *Boost Positivity* and the structured communication in *Kind Speech* to be effective.

The gratitude practice from the fourth book, *Build Inner Strength*, actively reinforces this physiological calming chemically. Gratitude acts as a natural stress detox, measurably reducing levels of cortisol, the primary stress hormone. Chronic elevation of cortisol is known to contribute to the negative neuroplasticity seen in anxiety and depression. By consistently lowering cortisol through daily practices, you are chemically supporting your body's move toward emotional equilibrium. A chemically calm brain is ready for positive growth.

The Mechanism of Neurocognitive Repair

The methods in this book actively target and correct the rigid information processing patterns that define chronic negativity.

1. **Breaking Cognitive Rigidity:** Negativity and depressive affect are characterized by fixed, predictable biases in memory, attention, and interpretation. The core CBT tools, like the Triple Column Technique, directly disrupt this rigidity. By forcing you to actively seek evidence that refutes a negative, automatic thought, you practice cognitive flexibility. This simple exercise strengthens your executive function, which is often weakened by persistent hostility and negativity .

2. **Sensitizing to the Good:** The Positive Neuroplasticity work, using the HEAL method, deliberately sensitizes your brain to "the good". Because sensitization is a general dynamic in the brain, repeated, intentional focus on positive feelings gradually makes your brain faster at registering and retaining beneficial experiences. This process actively reverses the negativity bias from the inside out.

3. **Restoring Behavioral Control:** Reactive anger is often associated with poor executive function, specifically deficits in behavioral inhibition . The pause created by the 4-7-8 breathing technique is a direct act of behavioral inhibition. This pause, the space between a stimulus and your impulsive reaction, re-engages your PFC. When you combine this physical control with cognitive strategies like structured problem-solving (Book 2), you develop alternative, functional strategies for responding to conflict . Empirical studies have demonstrated that these structured programs significantly increase problem-solving skills and decrease anger levels. This is not just learning to suppress anger; it is learning competence.

The Integration of Relational Skills

The third and fifth books provide the mechanism for applying your internal changes to the outside world.

Kind Speech provides the language of connection. Nonviolent Communication (NVC) is the core tool here. It shifts dialogue away from blame and judgment, replacing them with expressions of universal human needs, such as safety, connection, or understanding. By focusing on these shared human needs, the conversation transforms from a hostile confrontation into a collaborative search for solutions. The use of NVC measurably increases empathy and reduces interpersonal tension.

This structured communication is the mechanism for *Spread Respect*, the focus of the final book. Respect must be reciprocal. Social Exchange Theory helps you audit your relationships, ensuring the emotional costs and rewards are equitable. Self-respect is the foundation for this exchange.

Setting clear boundaries, a core action in Book 5, is the practical declaration of self-respect. Boundaries are the limits you establish to protect your mental health, energy, and time. Setting clear limits actively reduces the risk of burnout and prevents chronic energy depletion . When you communicate these boundaries assertively, using the skills learned in *Kind Speech*, you clearly define your value in the social exchange.

The most profound outcome of this entire guide is achieving personal integrity. Integrity means your external behavior consistently aligns with your core internal values. When your actions match your principles, you achieve an unshakable self-respect that commands the respect of others. This internal consistency is the final, durable shift: you move from reacting to the world to living intentionally, defined by resilience and mutually respectful connections.

This complete, five-part system ensures that your change is sustained and fundamental.

System	Goal	Neurocognitive Mechanism
Book 1: Boost Positivity	Rebuild flexible thought.	**Restores PFC function,** reverses negativity bias.
Book 2: Calm Anger	Restore physiological control.	**Engages Vagus Nerve,** increases HRV, and inhibits impulse.
Book 3: Kind Speech	Create clear, respectful dialogue.	**Trains mPFC / dlPFC** for cognitive empathy and social processing.
Book 4: Gratitude	Build chemical resilience.	**Reduces Cortisol,** strengthens reward circuits (compassion / caudate nucleus) .

System	Goal	Neurocognitive Mechanism
Book 5: Spread Respect	Enforce personal value.	**Establishes Integrity**, reducing stress caused by relational inequity.

This is your integrated action plan. It is time to start the work.

BOOK ONE
REWIRE YOUR BRAIN: ACTION STEPS TO BOOST POSITIVITY

INTRODUCTION
STEP OUT OF THE SHADOWS:
RECOGNIZING YOUR NEGATIVITY BIAS

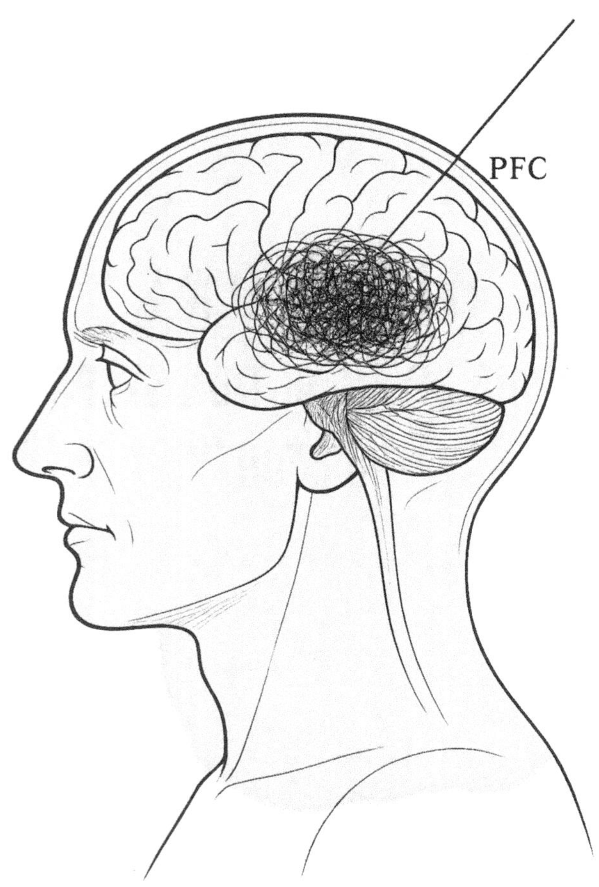

Let's talk about why you feel stuck in a loop of negative thinking. You've probably tried to "just be positive" before. Maybe you even told yourself to stop worrying. It did not work. This failure to simply choose happiness can make you feel weak or defeated. It can make you feel like negativity is a fixed part of who you are, a flaw in your character.

The truth is, your difficulty achieving a genuinely positive outlook is not a personal or moral failure. It is a predictable functional challenge. Your brain is not broken. It is simply wired according to an ancient set of priorities that no longer serve you.

This first chapter must change your basic understanding of your mind. You must realize that the problem is not *you*. The problem is the operating system running inside your head. Once you see the habit of negativity as a faulty program, you can begin the necessary work of rewriting the code.

The Biological Reality: Your Brain Clings to the Bad

The core mechanism driving constant pessimism is called the negativity bias. This is not a philosophical concept. It is a measurable biological default. Across various psychological situations and tasks, the adult brain exhibits an asymmetry: it has a propensity to attend to, learn from, and use negative information far more than positive information.

Think of your brain like a historian. If ten things happened today, nine good, one bad, your brain will spend more time reviewing the bad one. It learns more from it. It prioritizes the memory of it. This is why insults stick longer than compliments, and why criticism overrides success. Your brain is built with Velcro for the negative and Teflon for the positive.

For ancient humans, this bias was essential. Missing a positive opportunity, like a potential food source, was rarely fatal. But missing a threat, a poisonous snake, a predator, meant instant death. The negativity bias, therefore, served a critical, adaptive function, acting as an instant threat detection system that favored survival above all else. The brain that was overly cautious, worrying about every sound in the grass, lived long enough to reproduce.

In modern life, this mechanism is destructive. We live in environments where threats are chronic: financial stress, relational tension, work pressure, rather than acute, immediate physical dangers. Your brain, unable to distinguish between a deadline and a lion, activates the same hyper-alert, negative system. This sustained activation locks you into a state of anxiety and pessimism. It forces you to view your environment through a rigid, negative filter.

The Physical Toll of Chronic Stress

The belief that the world is dangerous and that you are inadequate to face it carries a high physical cost. Chronic psychological stress, fueled by the negativity bias, leads to measurable physical damage in your brain. This damage is known as negative neuroplasticity.

Studies show that chronic stress and depressive-like behaviors are associated with impairments in neuroplasticity. This includes observable neuronal atrophy and synaptic loss within key regions like the medial prefrontal cortex (mPFC) and the hippocampus.

Here is what that means in practical terms:

1. **Impaired Regulation:** Your emotional control center is the prefrontal cortex (PFC). The PFC is the wise leader of your brain, responsible for reason, planning, and regulating deep feelings. When stress damages the PFC, your ability to exert control, to stop, think, and choose a rational response, is functionally impaired.

2. **Hyperactive Alarm System:** Simultaneously, chronic stress causes the limbic system, particularly the amygdala, to become hyperactive. The amygdala is your brain's alarm bell. When the PFC is weakened and the amygdala is over-sensitized, the balance shifts. Impulse and fear override reason, leading to the rigid, inflexible thought patterns that characterize anxiety and depression.

You feel stuck in negativity because the physical structures necessary for flexible, positive thinking are temporarily weakened by stress. The goal of this entire book is to repair those structures and restore the PFC's rightful position as the regulator of your emotional life.

The Trap: Spotting Your Thinking Distortions

The negativity bias finds its expression in specific, predictable patterns of irrational thought called cognitive distortions, or cognitive errors. These are unhealthy thinking habits that fuel nearly all common mental health problems, including mood disorders and anxiety. They are not random errors. They are systematic ways your mind twists reality to fit your underlying negative assumptions.

The first step toward change is recognizing the structure of these traps. You must learn to separate the *thought* from the *fact*.

Common Thinking Errors:

Thinking Error	What it is	Example of the Distortion
All-or-Nothing Thinking	Seeing things in only extreme, absolute categories. There is no middle ground.	"I made one mistake on that report, so the whole project is a total failure."
Catastrophizing	Automatically predicting the worst possible outcome, believing the fear is fact.	"My partner is ten minutes late. They must have been in a terrible accident."
Mental Filter	Focusing only on the negative details of a situation while ignoring all positive ones.	You receive four positive reviews and one average review, but you only think about the average one.
Should Statements	Using rigid, moralistic rules about how you and others should behave.	"I *should* never feel tired," or "He *should* know better than to ask that."
Jumping to Conclusions	Interpreting events negatively without any definitive evidence. This includes mind-reading and fortunetelling.	"My boss didn't smile at me today, so I know she hates my work and is going to fire me."

When you believe these distortions, you fuel the negative cycles in your brain. For instance, when you engage in **Catastrophizing**, you are giving immediate, uncritical attention to a negative possibility. Because your brain is wired for threats, it treats that catastrophic thought as an immediate truth, intensifying the stress response and further weakening your emotional regulation.

The cycle sustains itself because these distorted thoughts become the fuel for chronic, negative mood states. Breaking this cycle demands a systematic approach. You cannot simply wish these habits away. You must scientifically test them and replace them with reality-based, balanced alternatives.

Many self-help approaches ask you to simply replace a negative thought with a positive affirmation. This method often fails because it ignores the neurobiological default. When you try to force positivity, the fragile positive thought immediately meets the negativity bias, which is the stronger, better-wired system. Your brain rejects the affirmation as fake or inauthentic because it is not based on actual, experienced, felt evidence. The negative system wins, and you feel worse.

The path to lasting change must leverage **positive neuroplasticity**. This concept confirms that just as negative habits can weaken neural connections, repeated beneficial mental habits can build new, positive structures. Your mind has the capacity to actively change your brain over time.

This work is about deliberate, structured effort to override the default setting. It is about creating sensitization for the good. If your brain is built with Velcro for the negative, we must teach it to grow Velcro for the positive. This requires turning momentary positive experiences into lasting neural changes.

Your Action Plan for Rewiring Your Brain

This book provides a systematic action plan to perform this repair and override your brain's negative default. We move through specific, measurable steps, using clinically validated techniques from CBT and modern neuroscience.

1. **Observation (Chapter 2):** You will use the Triple Column Technique to stop blindly accepting your thoughts as truth. You will learn to isolate the *momentary* negative thought and correctly diagnose the specific cognitive distortion that powers it. This recognition externalizes the problem. It allows you to address the bias as a faulty program separate from your core self-worth.

2. **Testing (Chapter 3):** You will treat your worst thoughts as scientific hypotheses, not as fixed facts. You will run behavioral experiments to gather real-world data that confirms or disconfirms your extreme thinking. This empirical approach shifts your internal narrative from fixed despair to observable data, strengthening the regulatory function of your PFC.

3. **Absorption (Chapter 4):** You will actively work against the negativity bias by training your brain to "take in the good." We will use the HEAL method to enrich and absorb beneficial experiences, hardwiring them into your neural structure. This creates resilience and boosts inner strength.

4. **Activation (Chapter 5):** We tackle the feeling of learned helplessness by emphasizing purposeful, structured action. By setting small, measurable goals and focusing on the process, you will restore striatal dopamine function and affirm your belief in personal agency, fighting back against inertia and burnout.

5. **Focus (Chapter 6):** You will use mindfulness and specific cognitive exercises, like Loving-Kindness Meditation, to train your attention away from the inner critic and toward self-compassion and acceptance.This practice actively strengthens your emotional resilience and provides internal peace.

The overall goal is simple: to make calmness, positivity, and flexible thinking your new, accessible default response. This change is not achieved by reading alone. It is achieved by doing. Every chapter provides a measurable action step designed to produce a measurable change in your mood, thoughts, and physiological state. Your new life begins with the decision to take back control of your own mental operating system.

CHAPTER 1

IDENTIFY THE TRAP:

SPOTTING YOUR THINKING DISTORTIONS

If the first chapter convinced you that your brain is simply running on outdated survival software, this chapter gives you the precise tool to debug that code. You cannot fight an invisible enemy. You have to make the destructive thoughts visible, label them correctly, and neutralize them with reason.

Most people treat their automatic thoughts, the internal dialogue that runs constantly, as absolute truth. If your brain says, "You messed that up, you always fail," you accept it as a statement of fact. This acceptance is the trap. These thoughts are not facts. They are predictable, repetitive, and often highly irrational errors in processing information, known as cognitive distortions.

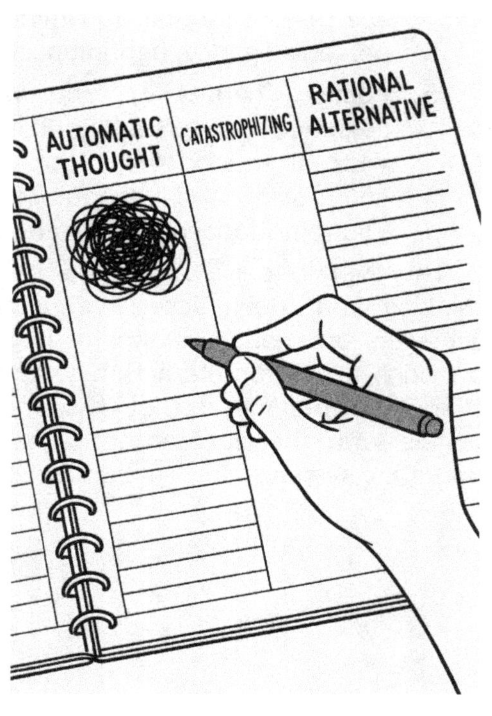

Identifying these specific, faulty patterns is the absolute cornerstone of Cognitive Behavioral Therapy (CBT). Until you learn to recognize the structure of your internal critic, you remain its servant.

The Triple Column Technique: A Scientific Audit

The most effective, accessible tool for dissecting these destructive thoughts is the Triple Column Technique (TCT). This method, developed by CBT psychologist David Burns, provides a systematic way to challenge and correct your most damaging thoughts. It moves the process from vague feeling to structured, empirical analysis.

To use the TCT, you physically create three columns on a sheet of paper or in a document. The purpose of this structure is to force your mind to slow down and process the thought rationally, rather than emotionally.

Column 1: The Automatic Negative Thought

The first step requires you to document the specific, automatic negative thought (ANT) that just crossed your mind, often triggered by an event, a conversation, or a setback. Capture the thought exactly as it occurred, without editing it for politeness or reason.

The goal here is total honesty. This is what your internal critic is saying.

- **Example Thought:** "I will never get my finances stabilized. I am completely hopeless and will end up alone."
- **Example Thought:** "My suggestion was rejected. That means I have no good ideas and people think I am stupid."

Column 2: The Cognitive Distortion (The Diagnosis)

This is the most critical column for long-term success. It is not enough to just write down the thought. You must correctly *diagnose* the type of thinking error you are committing.

By recognizing that the thought follows a predictable, irrational pattern, like **All-or-Nothing Thinking** or **Fortunetelling**, you externalize the problem. You stop seeing it as a reflection of your worth and start seeing it as an instance of a faulty program running in your brain. This recognition makes the thought easier to dismiss as invalid.

Here are the most common and damaging cognitive distortions that fuel negativity:

1. **All-or-Nothing Thinking (or Black and White Thinking):** This distortion forces you to see everything in absolute, extreme categories. If a performance is not perfect, it is a total failure. If a person is not always kind, they are entirely bad. There is no middle ground, no gray area, and no room for human error or nuance.

   - *Why it is damaging:* It leads to intense self-criticism and prevents you from acknowledging incremental progress or partial success. It fuels feelings of hopelessness because perfection is an impossible standard.
   - *Example Diagnosis:* The thought, "I made one mistake on that report, so the whole project is a total failure," is **All-or-Nothing Thinking**.

2. **Catastrophizing (or Fortunetelling):** This is the automatic prediction of the worst possible outcome. It involves treating the most frightening possibility as if it were a certain, imminent fact. It gives immediate, uncritical attention to a negative possibility.

   - *Why it is damaging:* It triggers the brain's ancient threat detection system. Your nervous system reacts as if the catastrophe were already happening, leading to sustained anxiety and preventing you from problem-solving logically.
   - *Example Diagnosis:* The thought, "My manager asked to speak with me later. I know they hate my work and I am going to be fired immediately," is **Catastrophizing** and **Fortunetelling**.

3. **Mind Reading:** This error is the assumption that you know what others are thinking without any factual evidence. You project your own anxieties and negative interpretations onto others.

   - *Why it is damaging:* It leads to unnecessary interpersonal conflict and self-sabotage. You react to your *assumption* of what they think, not to their actual words or intentions.

4. **Mental Filter:** This distortion involves focusing exclusively on the single negative detail in a situation while ignoring all positive elements. It is the definition of the negativity bias in action.

   - *Why it is damaging:* It maintains the negative cycle by starving your brain of the positive data it needs to build resilience. If you receive ten compliments and one criticism, the **Mental Filter** ensures you only remember the criticism.

5. **Disqualifying the Positive:** This is an active rejection of good experiences. A positive event is automatically dismissed as a fluke, dumb luck, or something that "doesn't count."

   - *Why it is damaging:* It prevents the necessary work of positive neuroplasticity. When you reject the good, you actively block your brain from learning from positive experience and changing its wiring.

6. **Should Statements:** These are rigid, critical rules you impose on yourself and others about how behavior *must* be. They often use words like *should, ought,* or *must.* When these rules are broken (as they inevitably are, because they are unrealistic), the result is intense guilt, frustration, and resentment.

- o *Why it is damaging*: They eliminate flexibility and compassion. They set an impossible, moralistic standard that prevents you from accepting reality as it is.

7. **Labeling:** This involves attaching a fixed, negative label to yourself or others based on a single action or mistake. Instead of saying, "I made a mistake," you say, "I am a total failure."

    - o *Why it is damaging*: Labels are self-fulfilling prophecies. They are global and absolute, defining your entire worth based on one imperfect moment.

By systematically identifying these errors, you gain distance from the thought. You realize: *This thought is not a truth. It is just an instance of the "All-or-Nothing" pattern.* This distance is where your emotional control starts to return.

Column 3: The Rational Alternative (The Correction)

The final step is to construct a balanced, factual, and rational alternative thought. This correction must not be a fake affirmation. It must be based on a cold, honest assessment of the evidence you have (or lack) in the real world.

This is the cognitive restructuring in action: replacing a stress-producing distortion with a balanced thought that does not produce anxiety.

To construct the Rational Alternative, you must ask yourself three key questions:

1. **What is the evidence that supports this thought, and what evidence refutes it?** Reviewing both sides forces a balanced, non-biased view.

    - o *Focus:* Look for actual facts, past successes, or instances where the negative belief did not come true.

2. **Are there alternative explanations for this event?** Generate explanations other than the original, negative, and self-blaming one.

    - o *Focus:* Could the manager have looked serious because they were focused on an urgent email? Could the friend have forgotten to invite you because they were genuinely busy?

3. **What are the realistic implications if the thought is true?** This question helps to determine the actual consequences, revealing that the outcome is rarely as catastrophic as initially feared.

- o *Focus:* If the thought is true, if your idea *was* bad, what is the worst realistic outcome? You propose a new idea next week. You do not lose your job or your self-worth.

Consistent application of the TCT disrupts the fundamental emotional pathways that fuel negativity. You must commit to using this as a daily habit, especially after high-stress or emotionally charged events.

Structured Practice Example

Column 1: Automatic Negative Thought (ANT)	Column 2: Cognitive Distortion	Column 3: Rational Alternative (Based on Evidence)
"My suggestion was rejected at the meeting. I have no good ideas. People think I am stupid."	**Labeling, Mental Filter, All-or-Nothing Thinking**	"It is true my idea was rejected. My coworker pointed out we lack the resources to implement it, which is an external factor, not a personal flaw. I often get complimented on my ability to think outside the box, and a few people even said they liked the concept. One rejection does not make me 'stupid' or mean I 'always' fail. I am capable and creative, and I will try a different approach next week."
"I missed my workout this morning. I am a lazy, undisciplined person and my health routine is ruined."	**Labeling, All-or-Nothing Thinking**	"I missed one workout, but I have gone five days this week. I am not 'lazy'; I am a person who sometimes misses a commitment. This routine is not 'ruined.' I will go this afternoon or start fresh tomorrow. I am disciplined most of the time."

Column 1: Automatic Negative Thought (ANT)	Column 2: Cognitive Distortion	Column 3: Rational Alternative (Based on Evidence)
"My partner hasn't replied to my text in two hours. They are deliberately ignoring me because they are secretly angry at me."	**Mind Reading, Catastrophizing**	"I do not know why they have not replied yet. They are likely in a meeting or driving. I felt anxious because I needed a connection, but I have no evidence they are angry. I will wait ten more minutes before I call. This is probably just a scheduling conflict."

Why Diagnosis Matters More Than Debate

The intermediate step, identifying the type of cognitive error, is the most crucial element for success. This is where the magic of CBT happens.

When you look at your thought and say, "Ah, that is just **Catastrophizing**," you immediately strip the thought of its power. You realize you are not facing an immediate threat; you are only facing a thought pattern. This recognition is why this technique is powerful for long-term change: it teaches you to catch yourself in the act of being irrational.

By recognizing the *pattern*, you are more likely to catch yourself and shift perspective.You stop paying uncritical attention to your inner critic and start treating it like a broken record player that keeps playing the same, old, inaccurate song.

Action Plan: Your Daily Cognitive Audit

To successfully rewire your brain, you must commit to a daily cognitive audit using the TCT.

Daily TCT Commitment:

1. **Capture the Worst Moments:** Carry a small notebook or use a notes app. Immediately after you feel a sudden surge of negative emotion, anger, anxiety, sadness, intense frustration, stop and capture the thought that generated the feeling in Column 1. Do this at least three times per day for the next week.

2. **Diagnose the Error:** Use the list of cognitive distortions to label the thought in Column 2. Try to find the single most accurate label, such as **Catastrophizing** or **All-or-Nothing Thinking**.

3. **Find the Facts:** Use the three guiding questions (Evidence, Alternatives, Implications) to build a rational, reality-based response in Column 3. The goal is to create a thought that is factual and therefore does not generate stress.

The sustained practice of this structured analysis actively weakens the rigid neural pathways associated with negativity. It restores your prefrontal cortex as the governing structure, allowing reason to regulate emotion. You are teaching your brain to prioritize reality over fear. This conscious, consistent effort is the first step in actively overriding the negativity bias and paving the way for positive, lasting change.

CHAPTER 2

RUN BEHAVIORAL TESTS: CHALLENGE YOUR WORST THOUGHTS

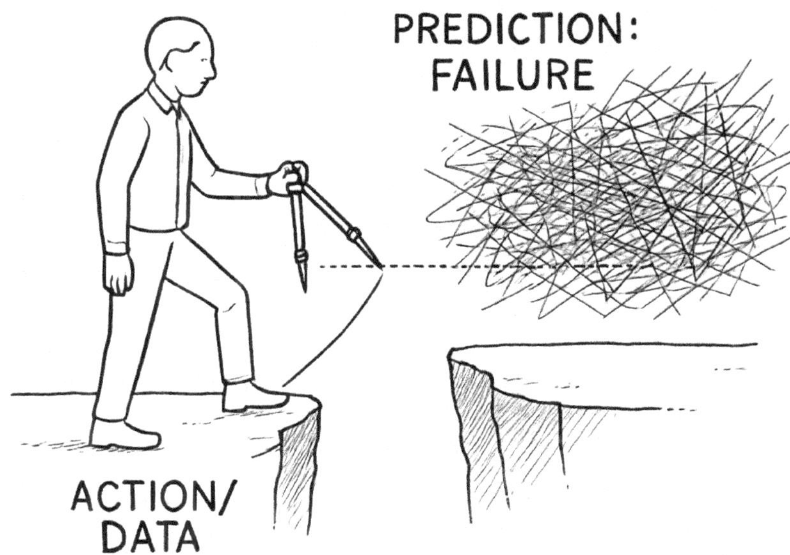

In the last chapter, you learned to stop accepting your thoughts as truth. You used the Triple Column Technique (TCT) to identify the specific errors: the **Catastrophizing**, the **Mind Reading**, the **All-or-Nothing Thinking** that fuels your negative emotional life. That was powerful intellectual work. You gained distance from the thought.

But distance is not destiny.

The next step is the crucial pivot. You must move from merely arguing with your thoughts internally to actively **testing** them in the real world. You have identified your faulty beliefs. Now you must treat them like a scientist treats a theory: **Thoughts are hypotheses, not facts.**

Your brain's negativity bias is a powerful, well-wired system. It will always win an internal debate against reason alone. To truly dislodge a core negative belief, you need undeniable, real-world data. You need to actively prove the old program wrong, and you do that through structured action called Behavioral Experiments (BEs).

The Flaw in Internal Argument

Why does simply debating with yourself often fail?

Imagine you firmly believe, "If I speak up in a meeting, everyone will think I am stupid." You can sit at your desk and argue: *That is a cognitive distortion. I have spoken up before. It is irrational to think I am stupid.* You might feel momentarily better. But the core belief is still active. The next time the situation arises, your body reacts with the same visceral fear, and the catastrophic thought returns with full power.

This happens because the belief is wired into your limbic system, your emotional core, and it has been reinforced thousands of times over years. Your PFC, the rational part of your brain, cannot simply override a deep, emotionally charged neural connection through logic alone. It needs empirical support.

Behavioral experiments are systematically designed tasks intended to generate that empirical evidence. They encourage you to gather data to confirm or disconfirm your extreme negative thinking. They are the most direct way to generate new, corrective experiences that your brain can accept as hard facts. This shift from internal argument to external, measurable action is what fundamentally changes your neural wiring.

Defining Behavioral Experiments

A Behavioral Experiment (BE) is a planned, purposeful action designed to test a specific, maladaptive belief about yourself, others, or the world.

Here is the essential distinction you must understand:

- **Pure Behavioral Exposure** aims to reduce emotional distress by allowing a conditioned fear response to extinguish. You repeatedly face a scary thing until you feel less anxious about it.

- **Behavioral Experiments** are explicitly designed to test the *accuracy* of a negative belief. The goal is cognitive change, the disconfirmation of the erroneous negative belief, using a real-world setting to collect data.

The power is in the design. You are not just doing a scary thing. You are designing a scientific task with a hypothesis, a methodology, and a plan for data analysis. The aim is to gather evidence that directly refutes the rigid, negative thought you identified in the TCT process.

Every effective Behavioral Experiment follows a structured, three-phase process. You must document these steps clearly.

Phase A: Articulate the Belief and Predict the Outcome (Hypothesis)

Before you act, you must write down the exact negative thought you are testing. Be specific. Global, vague thoughts ("I am a failure") are hard to test. Specific predictions are measurable.

1. **Identify the Core Belief (The Thought):** Go back to your TCT audit. Pick one distortion that consistently holds you back, such as **Catastrophizing** or **Mind Reading**.

2. **Formulate the Hypothesis (The Prediction):** State clearly, "If I do X, then Y will happen." Y must be the catastrophic outcome you fear.

Core Negative Belief	Hypothesis (Specific Prediction)
I am romantically undesirable, and people find me repulsive.	**Prediction:** If I ask someone I find attractive for a date, they will react with immediate disgust and disdain.
If I submit imperfect work, I will be immediately fired and humiliated.	**Prediction:** If I tell my supervisor I need one extra day on a deadline, they will angrily accuse me of laziness and threaten my job.

The clearer your prediction, the easier it is to measure the result. Assign a percentage of conviction to the prediction (e.g., "I am 85% certain they will be disgusted"). This provides a pre-experiment benchmark to measure the power of the disconfirmation later.

Phase B: Design the Test and Gather the Data (The Action)

Design a task that specifically targets the hypothesis in a safe, controlled way. The experiment must be achievable and directly challenge the belief.

1. **Design the Action:** What specific, measurable action will you take? *Example: If testing the fear of rejection, the action is asking one person out.*

2. **Define the Data:** What objective data will you collect? This is vital. You are not collecting *feelings*. You are collecting *facts*. *Example Data: The exact words the person used, their visible reaction, and the time the interaction took.*

3. **Plan for Safety/Mitigation:** What can you do if the outcome is negative? *Example: If they reject you, your mitigation plan is to immediately thank them for their time and walk away, upholding your self-respect.*

The action must be taken. This is non-negotiable. Even small, seemingly insignificant actions, like deliberately maintaining eye contact with three strangers for three seconds each, can be powerful tests against beliefs about social anxiety. You are actively gathering evidence to disprove the narrative of fear.

Phase C: Analyze the Result and Restructure the Belief (The Learning)

Once the experiment is complete, you must rigorously analyze the data you collected. This is where you use structured thinking to prevent the negativity bias from hijacking the result.

1. **Compare Data to Prediction:** Did the actual outcome match the catastrophic prediction? Be objective.

2. **Identify Disconfirmation:** Even if the result was negative (e.g., they said no to the date), did the *consequence* match the predicted *catastrophe* (disgust, humiliation)? A simple "no" disconfirms the predicted "disgust and disdain."

3. **Formulate the New Belief:** Based on the evidence, write a new, balanced, factual belief that replaces the old, distorted one.

During the analysis phase (Phase C), you use three key CBT questions to scrutinize the Automatic Negative Thought (ANT) against the real-world data. These questions force the brain out of the all-or-nothing trap and into nuanced, rational thinking.

1. What is the Evidence that Supports this Thought, and What Evidence Refutes it?

This is the central check for reality.

- **The Negative Thought (Hypothesis):** "I tried to delegate a task, and my coworker sighed. I am clearly an incompetent leader."

- **Evidence *For* the Thought:** The coworker sighed.

- **Evidence *Against* the Thought (Data):** The coworker immediately completed the task. They said, "Sure, I can do that." The sigh might have been related to the complexity of the task or an unrelated external stress (e.g., the heat in the room, their morning traffic). My manager gave me high marks for delegation last quarter.

Reviewing both sides forces you to hold a balanced perspective, acknowledging that the negative piece of data (the sigh) does not negate all the other evidence (the compliance, the competence history, the external factors). You use the facts to dilute the power of the feeling.

2. Are There Alternative Explanations for this Event?

The hostile attribution bias, closely linked to negativity, makes you assume negative, malicious intentions in ambiguous situations. This question forces you to broaden your perspective and stop jumping to conclusions (mind reading).

- **The Negative Thought (Hypothesis):** "My friend hasn't returned my text message. They are avoiding me because they are secretly angry at me."
- **Alternative Explanations (Data Review):** 1) They are in a meeting. 2) They left their phone charging. 3) They are driving. 4) They simply forgot. 5) They are dealing with a personal issue that has nothing to do with me.

By generating three to five realistic, neutral alternatives, you drain the emotional intensity from the original thought. The belief "They are angry at me" is no longer the only, or even the most likely, option. This move restores objectivity.

3. What are the Realistic Implications if the Thought is True?

This question directly attacks **Catastrophizing**. You assume, for the sake of argument, that the catastrophic thought is 100% true. Then you assess the *realistic* consequences.

- **The Negative Thought (Hypothesis):** "If I get a formal written warning from my job for being late, my career is completely ruined, and I will be homeless."
- **Realistic Implications:** If I get a written warning, I will be stressed. My career is not ruined; one warning is a chance to correct behavior. I am not at risk of immediate job loss or homelessness. The warning is a concrete signal to adjust my morning routine. I will feel embarrassed, but I will survive and fix the problem.

This process helps you determine the actual, manageable consequences, often revealing that the outcome, while uncomfortable, is not the terminal disaster you initially feared. You shift the focus from *fear* to *problem-solving*.

The Problem: David believes that when he attends a social event, everyone secretly judges his clothes, his job, and his quiet demeanor. He avoids making eye contact because he feels their critical gaze.

Phase A: Hypothesis and Conviction	Phase B: Designing the Test (The Action)	Phase C: Analysis and New Belief
Core Belief: Everyone at the party is critically judging me.	**Action:** David will attend a networking event for 30 minutes. His specific task is to make eye contact with five different people and ask them one neutral question (e.g., "How do you know the host?").	**Data Collected:** David made eye contact with 5 people. 3 returned the eye contact and smiled. 2 were focused on their own conversations and didn't notice him. 0 people pointed or laughed. The average interaction time was 45 seconds.
Prediction: If I look at people, they will recoil or openly stare back with contempt. **Conviction:** 90%	**Data to Collect:** Number of people who recoil / stare. Number of people who return a neutral / positive expression.	**Disconfirmation:** The prediction of contempt and recoiling was 100% disconfirmed. The actual data shows that people are either indifferent or slightly positive. The feeling of being watched was an internal projection (Mind Reading), not a factual occurrence.
	Mitigation: If he feels overwhelmed, David can retreat to the designated quiet corner for 5 minutes.	**New Belief:** "People at social events are primarily focused on their own conversations, not on judging my clothes. When I approach neutrally, I receive neutral or polite responses. My fear is a habit, not a fact."

The success of this experiment is *not* that David made five new friends. The success is that he disconfirmed the catastrophic nature of his prediction using empirical evidence. The data (three smiles, two people not noticing) directly refutes the thought "they stare with contempt." This correction is grounded in reality, making the new belief stronger than the old fear.

Application Case Study 2: Testing Performance Anxiety (All-or-Nothing Thinking)

The Problem: Sarah believes that because she needs help on a small part of a complex work project, she must be completely incompetent and will never succeed in her career.

Phase A: Hypothesis and Conviction	Phase B: Designing the Test (The Action)	Phase C: Analysis and New Belief
Core Belief: Needing help on a project equals total incompetence.	**Action:** Sarah will write an email to her most helpful teammate requesting specific assistance on one small component (a formula error in a spreadsheet). She must ask clearly and concisely.	**Data Collected:** The teammate replied 12 minutes later with the correct formula and added, "Thanks for asking, that formula is tricky." The supervisor was CC'd and did not reply at all. No one mentioned incompetence or laziness.
Prediction: If I ask for help, my teammate will call me incompetent, and my supervisor will lose all respect for me. **Conviction:** 75%	**Data to Collect:** Exact words of the teammate's response. Supervisor's visible reaction (if any). Time delay in response.	**Disconfirmation:** The prediction of being called incompetent and losing respect was completely disconfirmed. The actual data shows that asking for help was a normalized, non-catastrophic exchange that resulted in a solution. The negative outcome (total incompetence) did not occur.

| | **Mitigation:** If the teammate responds negatively, Sarah will remind herself that one rude response does not define her entire career or the entire team. | **New Belief:** "Asking for specific help on a small, tricky component of a project is normal, competent behavior that leads to effective problem-solving. My competence is defined by the full project delivery, not one formula error." |

The most important takeaway here is the cognitive shift. Sarah moves from the catastrophic belief ("I am incompetent") to the factual statement ("This formula is tricky"). She used action to prove that imperfection is not failure, disarming the **All-or-Nothing Thinking** that paralyzed her.

The Neuroplastic Power of Disconfirmation

You must understand why this action-oriented process is so effective at rewriting your brain's negative default.

Every time you successfully disconfirm a negative belief with real-world data, you weaken the neural connection that holds that belief. The initial connection (e.g., *speaking up = danger*) is a rigid pathway that has been reinforced over time. When you perform a Behavioral Experiment and the catastrophic outcome does not occur, your brain registers a cognitive error. The prefrontal cortex (PFC), your regulator, uses this objective data to challenge the validity of the old fear-based pathway.

- **Weakening the Old:** The old neural circuit linking the trigger (speaking up) to the catastrophic result (humiliation) weakens. The signal along that rigid path becomes less reliable.

- **Strengthening the New:** A new pathway is strengthened: the one linking the trigger (speaking up) to the factual, non-catastrophic result (solution, indifference, or a neutral response).

This is the power of empirical action. You are not just talking yourself out of a feeling. You are structurally changing the way your brain processes information, restoring the PFC's ability to exert reasoned, top-down control over the fear-processing limbic system. This is how you escape rigidity and cement genuine, lasting positive change.

You now possess the tools to audit your inner dialogue and challenge your fear-based beliefs. The TCT helped you label the enemy. The Behavioral Experiment forces you to defeat it with reality.

The entire foundation of emotional mastery rests on this empirical process. You must be willing to act, to risk a manageable failure, in service of gathering the objective data that will free you from the internal prison of negativity. The goal is to make the rational, balanced thought your most reliable, well-wired default response.

Your sustained, deliberate effort in applying these tools will shape your brain and make true, resilient positivity possible. The next step is learning how to actively capture and enrich the positive experiences that result from this new, confident action.

CHAPTER 3
FEEL THE GOOD: PRACTICING THE HEAL METHOD

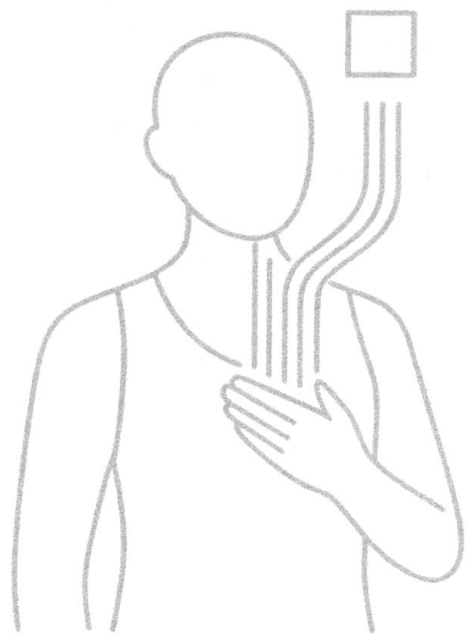

You have successfully learned to stop the bad. You used the Triple Column Technique (TCT) to identify the negative thought patterns, and you used Behavioral Experiments (BEs) to prove those fears wrong with real-world data. You now know that your catastrophic thinking is often irrational.

But simply removing the bad leaves an empty space. If you do not actively replace the old negative wiring with new, robust positive wiring, the old default system will eventually creep back in. Remember, your brain is still wired for the negativity bias; it clings to the bad and lets the good slide right off. We must fix this fundamental asymmetry.

This chapter introduces the science of *positive neuroplasticity*. It gives you a direct, actionable method to sensitize your brain to positive experiences and convert fleeting good moments into lasting emotional resources. This process is how you finally grow the "Velcro" for the positive feelings you want to keep.

The Problem: Teflon for the Good

Most people experience small, good moments every day: the comfort of a warm drink, a moment of connection with a friend, a small success at work, or a few minutes of quiet peace. We often notice these moments for a second, maybe two, and then our minds immediately jump back to a pressing problem, a worry, or a recent failure.

When this happens, you lose the opportunity to train your brain. For an experience to transition from short-term memory to long-term emotional storage, for it to become part of your emotional resource bank, it needs sustained attention. Because the negativity bias is so powerful, the brief positive moments are quickly filtered out and discarded, while the brain focuses intensely on perceived threats or losses.

Psychologist Rick Hanson's HEAL method is a practical, accessible, and evidence-based approach designed specifically to counteract this problem. It uses the power of your own mind to deliberately shape your brain over time through repeated positive mental habits. The goal is simple: turn states of mind into lasting, beneficial *traits*.

Early studies assessing this intervention found that people who used this method reported statistically significant self-reported improvements in happiness, resilience, savoring, and self-compassion. These results were often sustained for months, providing strong evidence that this technique fosters real, lasting neural change that builds emotional well-being.

The HEAL Protocol: Four Steps to Hardwire Happiness

The HEAL protocol involves four specific, actionable steps. You must dedicate a small amount of intentional time each day to move a positive experience through this sequence.

Step 1: Have a Good Experience (H)

The first step is simply noticing or creating a beneficial experience in daily life. This is not about finding a profound, life-altering moment. It is about registering small, everyday events that generate a feeling of contentment, connection, safety, or satisfaction.

Action Focus:

- **Look for the Small Wins:** Did you finish a difficult task? Did you manage to hold your tongue when you were provoked? Did a colleague genuinely thank you for your help?

- **Notice Sensory Comfort:** Focus on the simple experience of physical comfort: the feeling of warm water on your hands, the taste of a good meal, the sun on your skin, or the ease of soft clothing.
- **Acknowledge Inner Strength:** Recognize a momentary feeling of internal competence, moral clarity, or self-respect. If you successfully maintained a boundary from Book 5, that is a good experience to capture.

This step is an act of deliberate, positive selective attention. If you know you are going to record and enrich a positive moment, your brain naturally starts to scan your environment for those good things throughout the day, actively overriding the mental filter that usually focuses only on the negative.

Step 2: Enrich It (E)

This is the most crucial part of the process. Once you have a good experience, you must intensify and extend the positive thoughts and feelings associated with it. You are actively feeding the good experience to your brain's long-term memory system.

Action Focus:

- **Intensify the Feeling:** If the feeling is contentment, make it stronger. If it is pride, let yourself fully own that feeling of competence. Do not intellectualize it; *feel* it.
- **Focus on Sensory Details:** What are the sights, sounds, smells, and physical sensations connected to the experience? If you are enjoying a good conversation, notice the quality of the light, the tone of the other person's voice, and the relaxed feeling in your chest.
- **Extend the Time:** You must actively focus on the experience and its associated feeling for 10 to 30 seconds. This is the neurological consolidation time. Brief flashes of positive emotion are not enough; the sustained focus ensures the experience is registered as durable data by your neural structures.

The goal of this step is to move the positive experience from a fleeting event to a robust, rich, and detailed memory that is ready to be hardwired. This conscious dwelling prevents the Teflon effect.

Step 3: Absorb It (A)

In this phase, you intentionally allow the positive feeling to sink into your entire physical being. You move the experience from a thought in your head to a sensation in your body.

Action Focus:

- **Involve the Body:** Visualize the positive feeling; the warmth, the satisfaction, the peace, sinking deep into your core. Imagine it soaking into your chest, your heart, and your limbs.

- **Feel the Weight:** Notice where you feel the positive shift physically. Is there a softening in your jaw? A relaxation in your shoulders? A gentle warmth in your chest? Allow this physical sensation to build a lasting sense of contentment and self-compassion.

- **Let It Become You:** The goal is to merge the positive experience with your perception of self-worth and inner resources. It is not just "I saw a nice sunset." It is, "I am a person who is capable of feeling this deep sense of peace."

This step directly counteracts the negative neuroplasticity that chronic stress creates. By intensely and repeatedly focusing on positive feelings, you are strengthening the neural connections in your medial prefrontal cortex (mPFC), helping to repair the damage caused by chronic anxiety and self-judgment. You are actively restoring the physical integrity of your emotional regulatory system.

Step 4: Link It (L) - The Overriding Mechanism

This optional but powerful step moves the HEAL method into corrective therapy. The Linking step uses the newly absorbed positive strength to actively desensitize an older, milder negative experience or feeling.

This technique uses the new positive wiring to override the old negative wiring.

Action Focus:

- **Access the Negative:** Briefly recall a persistent, mild negative feeling, perhaps a small, lingering self-criticism or a minor anxiety about a future event. Do not choose an overwhelming trauma. Keep it small and manageable.

- **Bring the Positive to Bear:** Now, bring the rich, absorbed positive feeling (from Step 3) back to the forefront. Let the strong, positive sensation surround and integrate with the negative feeling.

- **Maintain Asymmetry:** The critical rule is that the positive feeling must always remain **"bigger and more powerful"** than the negative experience. If the negative feeling starts to overwhelm the positive one, immediately drop the negative focus and return to enriching the positive feeling (Step 2) until it is fully stable again.

This linkage gradually desensitizes your brain to the negative pattern, proving that the old feeling is not the only reality. You are teaching your neural pathways that the positive experience can successfully buffer, contain, and override the stress of the negative one. This is how you change a negative memory from one that drains your energy to one that is neutral or contained.

The Neuroplastic Power of Deliberate Savoring

The effectiveness of the HEAL method lies in its deliberate, sustained focus, which we call savoring. Savoring is the intentional act of prolonging and amplifying positive emotion. When you savor an experience for 20 seconds, you are activating and reinforcing the neural circuits associated with that positive emotion.

This process creates a functional change in your brain's structure:

1. **Strengthening the Regulator:** You are actively increasing the function of the PFC (your rational regulator) by giving it the job of focusing and sustaining attention on a positive stimulus. This top-down control strengthens its ability to manage impulse and fear.

2. **Sensitizing the Reward System:** By repeatedly enriching and absorbing positive feelings like contentment and self-compassion, you are sensitizing your brain's reward circuits. You are making your brain more responsive to happiness and less reliant on external threats to grab its attention.

This training moves you toward a state of *metaplasticity*, an activity-dependent, persistent change in the neural state that shapes the direction, duration, and magnitude of future synaptic change. In simple terms, you are not just making yourself happy today. You are making yourself more capable of happiness tomorrow.

Action Plan: Your Daily HEAL Practice

To successfully integrate positive neuroplasticity, you must commit to a daily practice. This should be done multiple times per day for short, intense bursts, not one long, abstract session.

1. **Set Your Intention:** Decide you will HEAL three small experiences today, one during your morning routine, one during the workday, and one in the evening.
2. **Execute the Steps:** When a positive moment occurs:
    - **H (Have it):** Notice it immediately.
    - **E (Enrich it):** Focus on the physical feeling and the sensory details for at least 15 seconds. Make it intense.
    - **A (Absorb it):** Visualize the feeling sinking deep into your body and becoming part of your inner strength.
3. **Use Linking Strategically:** Use the Linking step only when you have a strong, contained positive feeling and you are targeting a very mild, manageable negative thought or memory. Always prioritize strengthening the positive feeling first.

By applying the HEAL method, you stop relying on luck or circumstance for your mood. You seize control of the information that enters your brain, ensuring that every small success, comfort, or moment of peace is absorbed and converted into durable, resilient inner strength. You are no longer just surviving your life. You are actively building your mind.

CHAPTER 4
BUILD YOUR AGENCY:
USE ACTION TO CREATE HOPE

You have done the foundational work. You have identified the cognitive traps using the TCT, and you have started testing those false beliefs against reality using Behavioral Experiments. You are now intellectually aware of your negativity bias.

But knowledge alone does not guarantee freedom.

Most people reach this point and stop. They understand the patterns but still cannot seem to *act*. They recognize the illogical nature of their fear, yet they remain immobilized by inertia, procrastination, and a profound sense of "stuckness."

This is the central issue we address now: the collapse of motivation. If you feel immobilized, if you constantly struggle to start tasks or feel an overwhelming sense of futility, you are experiencing a state called **learned helplessness**. It is a condition of conditioned loss of effort that is rooted in your neurochemistry, not your character.

This chapter is the instruction manual for overriding that feeling. The scientific solution is simple and profound: **Action restores hope.** We use deliberate, purposeful action to chemically restore your brain's motivation and reward circuit, fundamentally reversing learned helplessness. You will learn to use structured action as your primary psychological intervention.

The Neuroscience of Inertia: When Dopamine Drops

We must first look beneath the feeling of low motivation. The sense of inertia, burnout, and hopelessness you feel is directly linked to chronic exposure to psychosocial stress or adversity.

When you face repeated stressors, such as financial instability, relational conflict, and constant self-criticism, without perceiving any control over them, the brain registers a profound lack of agency. This perception of futility has a measurable chemical result: **dampened striatal dopamine synthesis.**

1. **The Reward Circuit Goes Offline:** Dopamine is the critical neurotransmitter associated with motivation, pleasure, and reward. It is the "wanting" signal that pushes you to seek goals and solve problems. The striatum is the key area for motivation and reward.

2. **Stress Silences Motivation:** Long-term exposure to stress or adversity causes the brain to make less dopamine in the striatum. When the brain's reward circuits go offline, motivation and interest diminish. This is exactly what burnout feels like. You do not lack willpower; you lack the necessary neurochemical drive to start.

3. **Learned Helplessness Takes Hold:** This state describes the conditioned loss of effort. Even when an opportunity for success or escape presents itself, the brain remains still, stuck in learned inertia because it believes that effort will not produce a result.

The paralysis you feel is a reversible brain state. It is a chemical pattern that has taken hold due to overwhelming stress, not a permanent failure of your inner drive.

The Reversal: Action Restores Agency

The solution to learned helplessness is behavioral activation. You must engage in consistent, purposeful action that produces a real, observable result.

The mechanism for recovery is rapid and direct. When you take an action and perceive that your output yields a result, a successful step toward a goal, dopamine levels in the ventral tegmental area (VTA) rise almost immediately. This chemical affirmation reinforces your belief in personal agency: *What I do matters.* This immediate feedback loop restores the brain's reward circuit and affirms that effort is worthwhile.

This principle is the foundation of **Action-Oriented Therapy.** This approach is evidence-based and emphasizes taking concrete, specific actions to improve well-being and overcome challenges.

- **Move Beyond Talk:** Action-oriented therapy goes beyond traditional talk therapy. It focuses on identifying negative patterns and beliefs, then immediately encourages the client to take *specific actions* that lead to positive change.

- **The Empowerment Loop:** Taking purposeful action, whether small or large, creates an immediate sense of empowerment and confidence in your ability to shape your life. For individuals prone to procrastination or feeling immobilized, this practical, solution-focused method is highly effective.

The change you are seeking is generated when you move from intellectual contemplation to physical, measurable action. You are not waiting to feel motivated before you act. You are acting *to generate* motivation.

The Toolkit: Structured Goal Setting for Momentum

To ensure your action successfully generates the necessary dopamine response, it must be structured and measurable. Vague goals like "be better" or "be happier" are useless. They do not provide the brain with the clear signal needed to register success.

The standard for setting goals that generate momentum is the **SMART** framework. These goals are designed to be practical, solution-focused, and, crucially, measurable to affirm agency.

1. Specific: Define Exactly What You Will Do

The action must be precisely defined. Avoid ambiguity. The brain needs a clear finish line to celebrate the successful effort.

- *Vague:* "I will work on my finances."

- *Specific:* "I will spend 30 minutes on Tuesday evening creating a budget spreadsheet and logging my expenditures from the last two weeks."

2. Measurable: Quantify the Effort and Result

The action must have a number attached to it, time, duration, quantity, or frequency. This allows the brain to register objective success, which triggers the dopamine reward.

- *Vague:* "I will start writing my paper."
- *Measurable:* "I will write one full page (approximately 300 words) of my paper today before 5:00 PM."

3. Attainable: Start Small to Guarantee Success

This is the most critical step for reversing learned helplessness. Your initial actions must be intentionally small and easily achievable. You are not aiming for your life's greatest achievement; you are aiming for a guaranteed win.

The problem with feeling stuck is that the brain believes failure is guaranteed. You must override this belief with repeated, undeniable success.

- If your core goal is to clean your entire apartment, your attainable action is to spend **ten minutes cleaning only the kitchen counter**.
- If your core goal is to start running, your attainable action is to **put on your running shoes and walk outside for five minutes**.

These small, purposeful actions immediately trigger dopamine release and restore agency. They affirm that your effort can, in fact, produce a result, no matter how small. This restores motivation and builds the momentum required for larger tasks later.

4. Relevant: Align Action with Core Values

The action must align with a deeper, core reason for change, the personal values that guide your decisions (as we will explore in Book 5). When action is relevant to your self-respect or health, the reward is greater.

- *Action:* "I will spend 45 minutes organizing my chaotic desk."
- *Relevance:* "I am doing this because order promotes mental clarity, and mental clarity aligns with my core value of competence and focus."

5. Time-based: Set a Clear Deadline

Set a definitive start and finish time for the task. This creates a structure and reduces the cognitive load associated with decision-making. Knowing when the effort stops makes starting easier.

- *Action:* "I will review my emails and flag the three most urgent ones."
- *Time-based:* "I will complete this review by 9:30 AM today."

The Momentum Engine: Targeting the Positive Affect System

The benefits of structured action extend beyond simply completing tasks. Action is a powerful tool for generating positive emotion and fundamentally changing how you feel.

Targeting the positive affect system through structured action generates substantial improvements in positive emotions and overall well-being. Research shows that multicomponent psychological interventions focused on positive affect are highly beneficial. They generate improvements in positive emotions and well-being, while simultaneously reducing negative affect and symptoms of anxiety or depression.

How Action Boosts Affect:

1. **Sense of Accomplishment:** Completing a task, even a small one, is an objective success. This feeling of competence directly counters the feelings of inadequacy and hopelessness that fuel learned helplessness.

2. **Interruption of Rumination:** When you are engaged in active, structured problem-solving, you are physically unable to dwell on negative rumination. Rumination, the repetitive focus on a stressful event, physiologically sustains your body's stress response, predicting slower heart rate recovery and heightened anxiety. Action forces your brain to shift its focus from replaying the past to constructively engaging with the present.

3. **Physical Release:** Action is often physical. Even organizing a desk or taking a five-minute walk releases tension and redirects energy that might otherwise be stored as stress or irritability.

By integrating action into your recovery, you are providing your brain with the corrective experience it needs to rebuild its reward system. This process is solution-focused, practical, and highly effective for individuals who previously felt paralyzed by procrastination or sadness.

Action Plan: Generating Hope Through Small Wins

Your task now is to design and execute three small, high-leverage actions this week. These actions must be designed to guarantee a success, no matter how minor, to rebuild your dopamine feedback loop.

Step 1: Identify an Inertia Point

Where do you consistently feel stuck? Is it initiating work? Starting a conversation? Cleaning a specific area? Choose one small area where the feeling of helplessness is strong.

- *Example Inertia Point:* I keep putting off responding to one specific, annoying email.

Step 2: Apply the SMART Framework

Turn the inertia point into a guaranteed win.

SMART Element	Application	Result
Specific	Write the draft email reply outlining the next steps.	A completed draft.
Measurable	I will spend **15 minutes max** on this task.	Time boxed effort.
Attainable	I will only draft it; I do not have to send it yet.	Low pressure, high completion chance.
Relevant	This action aligns with my value of **professional competence** and **clarity**.	Increased self-respect.
Time-based	I will start at 4:00 PM today.	Clear start time.

Step 3: Track the Neurochemical Result

After you complete the 15-minute action, pause and engage in immediate self-reflection:

1. **Assess Agency:** On a scale of 1 to 10 (10 being high), how strongly do you believe your effort produced a tangible result? (The number should be high.)

2. **Note Physical Shift:** Where did you feel the shift in your body? Was the knot in your stomach a little looser? Did your mind feel quieter?

3. **Acknowledge Dopamine:** State the success clearly: "I successfully started and completed the draft email within the time limit. My effort worked. I restored agency."

This deliberate acknowledgment of the small win is what cements the positive neuroplastic change. It proves to your brain that the cycle of inertia is broken, and that you are in charge again.

The Integration of Action: Cementing All Five Skills

The move to action is not just a chapter in a book; it is the engine that drives the entire five-part system.

- **Action and Positivity (Book 1):** Successful action provides the real-world, positive data needed to fuel your Behavioral Experiments and the HEAL method. When you achieve a small win, you have a concrete, positive experience to enrich and absorb.

- **Action and Anger (Book 2):** Problem-solving skills, which are action-oriented, are essential for effective anger management. Structured action provides an alternative strategy for responding to conflicts, moving you away from impulsive reaction toward thoughtful, planned response.

- **Action and Regulation:** Most importantly, consistent action strengthens your prefrontal cortex (PFC). Every time you choose to pursue a SMART goal instead of passively succumbing to inertia, you are exercising the PFC's regulatory capacity. This sustained effort structurally repairs the neurological damage caused by chronic stress, reinforcing all the other skills you are building, from emotional regulation to assertive communication.

Action, therefore, is not a bonus skill. It is the necessary bridge between a stuck, negative life and one defined by hope, clarity, and competence. You cannot wait for the feeling. You must commit to the steps. Your brain will follow.

CHAPTER 5
TRAIN YOUR FOCUS:
REDIRECTING ATTENTION TO THE POSITIVE

You are now engaged in a two-part process of transformation. First, you are dismantling the old structure of negativity by testing your distortions and forcing action. Second, you are actively building the new structure by converting fleeting positive experiences into lasting neural traits using the HEAL method.

The next critical step is training your attention itself. Your attention is the steering wheel of your consciousness, and where it goes, your energy, and your neuroplastic changes, follow. Since your brain is built to prioritize negative input, you must deliberately train your focus to seek, register, and dwell on positive data. This is not passive wishing; it is an active cognitive skill that strengthens your emotional resilience and self-worth.

We will focus on two key, evidence-based practices that redirect your inner focus: **Mindfulness** for detachment and **Loving-Kindness Meditation (LKM)** for cultivating self-compassion. This combination interrupts the inner critic and replaces self-judgment with acceptance.

The inner critic is the voice that interprets a mistake as a moral failing, that defaults to judgment, and that disqualifies positive experiences. This voice is powerful because it is reinforced by the rigidity of your cognitive distortions (like **Labeling** and **All-or-Nothing Thinking**) and the innate power of the negativity bias. The inner critic is the primary source of self-judgment, which creates stress and actively impedes the repair work you are doing in your prefrontal cortex (PFC).

If you cannot silence the critic, you cannot achieve lasting inner peace. The solution is not to fight the voice, which often makes it louder. The solution is to change your *relationship* with the voice, recognizing it as a collection of thoughts, not as your identity.

Tool 1: Mindfulness for Detachment

Mindfulness is a state of conscious awareness where you intentionally focus on the present moment, acknowledging thoughts, feelings, and bodily sensations without judgment. It is a tool for detachment.

When a negative thought arises ("I am lazy," "I should have done better"), your typical response is to immediately fuse with that thought: you believe it and react emotionally. Mindfulness creates a necessary space between you and the thought.

Action Focus: Non-Judgmental Observation

1. **Stop and Notice:** When the negative thought appears, physically stop what you are doing. Do not react.

2. **Label the Thought:** Without judgment, simply label the thought as a *mental event*. Say, "I am having the thought that I am lazy," or "That is a familiar voice of **Labeling**." This act of labeling separates the thought from reality.

3. **Allow the Thought to Pass:** Imagine the thought as a cloud passing in the sky or a car driving past you. Do not invite it in for tea. Simply observe it and allow it to continue on its path.

This practice is essential because it is activity-dependent. Repeatedly observing negative thoughts without reacting to them weakens the automatic neural response. You are literally training your brain to stop prioritizing the emotional signal sent by the inner critic. Mindfulness allows you to detach from the thoughts, viewing them as temporary mental events rather than absolute, fixed truths.

Once you have detached from the negative thought, you need a positive replacement. This is where **self-compassion** comes in.

Self-compassion is the intentional direction of warmth, kindness, and understanding toward yourself, especially during moments of perceived failure or suffering. It is treating yourself with the same support and kindness you would offer a cherished friend. This practice is crucial for overriding the inner critic and building resilience.

Clinically, self-compassion is proven to work. Studies show that structured exercises focused on self-compassion successfully reduce self-judgment and substantially enhance self-worth and emotional well-being. This is not just a kind feeling; it is a direct cognitive intervention that promotes long-term change.

The most effective, evidence-based method for cultivating this inner warmth is **Loving-Kindness Meditation (LKM)**.

Loving-Kindness Meditation (LKM) Protocol

LKM is a structured thought exercise that uses the repetition of specific phrases to generate and direct feelings of warmth and acceptance, first toward yourself, then toward others.

Action Focus: Directing Kindness Inward

1. **Find Calm (Breathing):** Start by taking a few slow, diaphragmatic breaths (the calming techniques from Book 2, such as 4-7-8 breathing, are perfect here). This downregulates your stress level and slows your thoughts, creating the mental space for the LKM to work.

2. **Target the Self:** Begin by silently repeating a set of self-compassionate phrases. Use an open posture, hands resting gently on your lap, or one hand on your chest, to reinforce the physical sense of warmth.

   o Example Phrases:

     - "May I accept myself as I am right now."
     - "May I be safe and protected from harm."
     - "May I be peaceful and at ease."
     - "May I be kind to myself at this moment."

3. **Visualize Acceptance:** As you repeat these phrases, visualize the feeling of warmth, acceptance, and self-worth sinking into your body. Feel the warmth filling the spaces where tension or self-

criticism usually resides. The goal is to generate and sustain the positive emotional response for several minutes.

Why LKM Works Neurochemically:

LKM does more than just make you feel warm. By directing compassion inward, you are engaging and strengthening key neural circuits. Compassion, the desire to alleviate suffering (whether your own or others'), is associated with activity in brain regions linked to the reward system, specifically the right caudate nucleus.

Individuals who display lower levels of compassion often show reduced neural activity or gray matter volume in these reward areas. By repeatedly practicing LKM, you are strengthening these reward circuits, making self-compassion intrinsically motivating and reinforcing. You are building resilience against the inner critic by chemically rewarding the choice of acceptance over judgment.

Training Your Focus: The Practice of Positive Sensitization

Beyond formal meditation, you must actively train your attention throughout the day to prioritize positive data, a process called positive sensitization. Since the brain operates on a mechanism of sensitization, repeated activation makes neural circuits more responsive. If you repeatedly focus on negativity, the circuit for worry gets faster. If you focus on the good, the circuit for joy gets faster.

This practice works directly with the HEAL method from Chapter 4. It ensures that you are not just having a good experience but are actively increasing the speed and efficiency with which your brain registers and holds onto it.

Action Focus: Intentional Positive Scanning

1. **Micro-Acknowledge Successes:** Make a practice of stopping for 5 seconds when you complete any task, even a small one. Instead of immediately moving to the next thing, acknowledge: "I finished that. I am competent." This stops the negative momentum and provides a concrete piece of positive data.

2. **Seek Out Neutral/Positive Data:** When walking through a store, driving, or sitting in a park, consciously train your focus to look for things that are neutral or pleasant, rather than things that generate irritation or stress. Notice the color of the sky, the sound of the traffic flowing smoothly, or the simple fact that your basic needs (safety, warmth, food) are currently met. This is a deliberate counter-measure against the negativity bias filter.

3. **Anchor with the Body:** Whenever you register a positive feeling, quickly connect it to a physical sensation, as you learned in the HEAL method (Chapter 4). Notice the relaxation in your muscles or the warmth in your hands. This physical anchoring makes the positive experience more robust and easier for the brain to absorb, further reducing self-judgment.

Through consistent practice, these structured thought exercises actively rewire your brain to respond to challenges with self-acceptance rather than criticism. This systematic redirection of attention creates a neural default toward resilience and self-worth.

The Integration of Regulation

Mindfulness and LKM are not isolated practices. They are crucial supports for the entire five-book system.

- **Supporting Cognitive Restructuring (Chapter 2, 3):** Mindfulness creates the necessary space to observe your Automatic Negative Thoughts (ANTs) without reaction, making it easier to step back and apply the TCT. You need to be detached from a thought to successfully question its evidence.

- **Supporting Physiological Calm (Book 2):** Diaphragmatic breathing, the foundation of LKM, supports the downregulation of stress, which is the cornerstone of managing anger. This physiological calm makes it possible to maintain cognitive and emotional control in difficult moments.

- **Building Agency (Chapter 5):** When you approach a task with self-compassion instead of self-judgment, you are less likely to fall into the paralyzing trap of **All-or-Nothing Thinking**. You accept that effort is enough and that imperfection is expected. This compassionate approach lowers the pressure and makes it easier to initiate the action needed to restore dopamine and break learned helplessness.

Your sustained commitment to training your focus is the final, essential step in this book. You are seizing control of your inner narrative. You are replacing the inner critic with a wise, compassionate ally. This internal peace is the most powerful resource you can possess, ensuring that the positive changes you have made are durable and self-sustaining.

Commit to integrating these attention-training tools into your daily routine.

Part A: Mindfulness & Detachment

1. **Daily Audit:** For the next three days, when you feel acute frustration or self-judgment, immediately pause. Write down the negative thought, and then simply observe it for 60 seconds without judgment.

2. **Label the Source:** If the thought is a critique, label it as "The Critic." If it is a prediction, label it as "**Fortunetelling**." This is the core act of detachment.

Part B: Loving-Kindness Meditation (LKM)

1. **Commitment:** Practice LKM for five uninterrupted minutes every morning before starting your day.

2. **Script:** Start with the self-compassion phrases: "May I accept myself as I am. May I be safe. May I be peaceful. May I be kind to myself."

3. **Physical Anchor:** Focus on where you feel the warmth and peace in your body. Allow the positive sensation to linger after the exercise is finished, anchoring the feeling of self-worth into your physical being.

By actively training your focus toward compassion and positive sensitization, you are giving your brain the consistent input it needs to make positivity your new default. You are teaching your mind that you are worthy of kindness, acceptance, and peace. This foundation of self-respect makes every other skill in this guide possible.

CONCLUSION
CEMENTING POSITIVE CHANGE: YOUR NEW NEURAL DEFAULT

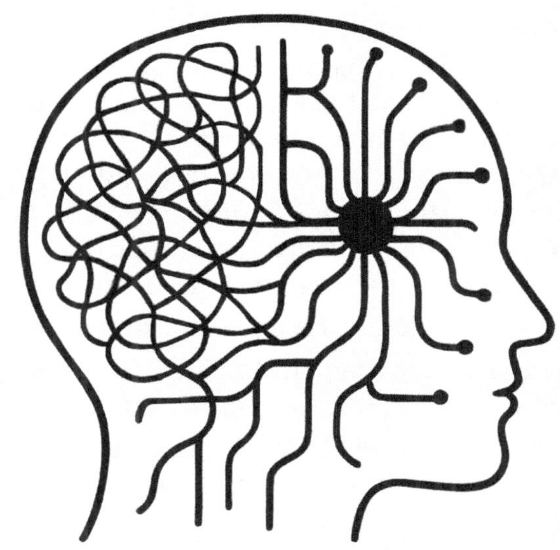

You've now gone through a complete cycle of inner repair. This book, Rewire Your Brain, guided you through a hands-on, practical look at your inner world. You started by realizing your brain tends to default to negative thoughts. Now, you've actively installed new, positive ways of thinking. This final chapter focuses on making that change strong and lasting, so flexible thinking, self-kindness, and control become your brain's new, resilient norm.

Let's quickly revisit the three key steps you took: Analyze, Activate, and Absorb. When you keep using these steps, they tap into neuroplasticity, your brain's way of changing its structure, letting you hold onto emotional balance and confidence for the long haul.

Reviewing the Process: Analyze, Activate, Absorb

What makes this change powerful is how systematic it is. You didn't just try to "think happy thoughts." Instead, you followed a proven method to repair your thinking and brain patterns.

1. Analyze: Breaking Down Rigid Thinking

You began by carefully spotting mistakes in your thinking with the Triple Column Technique (TCT). This was key to moving past rigid thinking, the trap of only seeing events through your immediate feeling, which lies at the heart of negative emotions.

The Action: You treated your thoughts like guesses, not facts. By naming a thought "Catastrophizing" or "Mind Reading," you stepped outside the problem. You understood it was a faulty program running, not a true reflection of your value.

The Brain Effect: This sharp analysis strengthened your brain's thinking center (the Prefrontal Cortex or PFC). You taught the PFC to take charge and calm emotional reactions from the limbic system. This restored your brain's top-down control over emotions.

Next, you did a vital step: testing your fears in real life with Behavioral Experiments (BEs). You found your worst predictions rarely came true. This weakened the old fear pathways in your brain.

2. Activate: Taking Back Control and Building Momentum

Moving into action, covered in Chapter 5, aimed straight at the paralyzing feeling of helplessness that feeds burnout.

The Action: You set small, SMART goals, things you could easily succeed at, like ten minutes of tidying, a page of writing, or one clear conversation. This kicked you out of stuckness.

The Brain Chemistry: Success sparked a quick dopamine boost in the striatum. Dopamine fuels motivation and reward. This showed your effort counts, restoring your belief in personal power and lighting up your brain's reward system. Taking action also breaks the cycle of rumination, the harmful looping over past stress, helping you live in the present again.

3. Absorb: Building Resilience and Self-Worth

Finally, you trained your brain to turn good moments into lasting strength. You flipped the brain's negativity bias.

The Action: Using the HEAL method, you made sure to **Have, Enrich, and Absorb** positive experiences for 10 to 30 seconds. This savoring moved good feelings from brief moments to long-lasting brain connections, a kind of positive rewiring.

The Brain Effect: This practice reinforced brain areas that control emotions and resilience, fighting damage from chronic stress. By focusing on positives, you helped your brain get better at noticing and holding onto peace and self-worth. You also practiced Loving-Kindness Meditation (LKM), proven to lower self-judgment and boost self-compassion by activating the brain's reward circuits.

Lasting Change: From Temporary State to Permanent Trait

The goal is to turn positive feelings into a solid part of who you are, not just a passing mood. This happens through metaplasticity: a process where your brain's state changes dependently on your activities, affecting all future learning and wiring.

You've made the positive path the easiest one for your brain to follow by consistently challenging thoughts with TCT, taking action regularly, and absorbing peace with HEAL. Resilience isn't about dodging problems; it's about bouncing back quickly after setbacks.

When challenges come:

- You spot distorted thinking quickly because TCT is strong.
- You regain calm faster since your PFC controls emotions better thanks to action.
- You find positive support swiftly because HEAL built a foundation of safety and worth.

Looking Ahead: What Comes Next

The stability you built here is the foundation for everything else. The mental clarity and regained power you gained are key for upcoming work on relationships:

- Without a calm PFC (Book 1), managing strong impulses like anger (Book 2) is tough.
- Without clear thinking and control (Book 1), asking for what you need kindly (Book 3) is harder.
- Without noticing good things (HEAL), you can't fully benefit from gratitude and connection (Book 4).
- Without self-kindness (LKM), setting healthy boundaries (Book 5) becomes tricky.

The work is inward and deeply personal. Now, with a rewired brain, you're ready to face perhaps the biggest challenge to your well-being and relationships: uncontrolled anger. The next book will guide you from volatile reactions to real control over your feelings and actions.

Your new neural habit is set. You are no longer defined by old patterns.

REFLECTION QUESTIONS

1. Name three common distorted thoughts you spotted in your journals this month. What facts or balanced thoughts helped prove them wrong?

2. When did you feel stuck by helplessness this week? What small SMART action did you take? What immediate change did you notice emotionally or chemically?

3. How did you use HEAL to savor a good experience today? Which body sensation did you link to that feeling, and how long did you hold it?

4. When was your inner critic loudest? How did you use LKM or mindfulness to step back from judgment and be kinder to yourself?

5. Thinking about your Behavioral Experiments, what strong evidence did you find that a core fear (rejection, failure, humiliation) was an inaccurate prediction?

BOOK TWO
TAKE BACK CONTROL:
TECHNIQUES TO CALM ANGER NOW

INTRODUCTION

ANGER IS INFORMATION:

UNDERSTANDING THE CYCLE OF RAGE

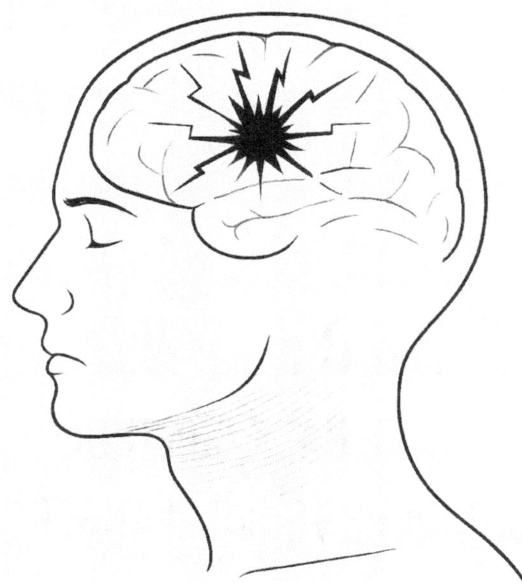

You have successfully stabilized your internal narrative in Book 1. You understand that negativity is a faulty program you can overwrite. But when anger hits, that sudden, hot surge in your chest, the tightness in your jaw, the rapid, judgmental thoughts, all that cognitive work can instantly dissolve. Anger is visceral. It bypasses reason. It makes you feel out of control, not because you lack discipline, but because your body has initiated a complex, ancient physiological response that overrides the rational brain.

If you struggle with anger, you know the cost firsthand. It pushes away the people you value, damages your credibility, and leaves you feeling exhausted and ashamed. Trying to manage it by simply suppressing it is a dead end. Suppression leads to its own set of damaging outcomes, including reduced relationship quality and increased risk for conditions like coronary heart disease and chronic pain. Your body pays a price for that internalized hostility.

This book is dedicated to mastering that physical and emotional surge. We stop seeing anger as a moral failure and start treating it as **information**, a powerful, often distorted signal that an underlying need is unmet or a perceived threat is present. The key to lasting change is understanding that the most effective interventions occur *before* anger reaches the boiling point, when you can still access the skills you learned in Book 1.

The Biology of the Blow-Up: From Signal to Surge

Anger is not purely emotional. It is a full-body, neurochemical event: the activation of your sympathetic nervous system, also known as the fight-or-flight response.

When your brain perceives a threat, whether it is a genuine physical danger or a verbal slight at work, your amygdala, the brain's alarm bell, initiates a cascade of chemical events:

1. **Chemical Release:** Stress hormones like cortisol and adrenaline flood your system. Your heart rate accelerates, breathing becomes shallow and rapid, and blood is diverted from your digestive organs and rational brain (the PFC) toward your large muscle groups, preparing you to fight or run.

2. **Cognitive Shutdown:** Because blood is diverted, the prefrontal cortex (PFC), the region responsible for reason, logic, and emotional regulation, loses resources. In short, the rational part of your brain goes momentarily offline. This is why you say and do things in the heat of the moment that you immediately regret, you literally cannot access your best judgment.

3. **Physical Warning Signs:** This physiological arousal creates immediate, measurable physical changes. You might feel a rapid heart rate, muscle tension (especially in the jaw, neck, and shoulders), flushed skin, or a sudden burst of energy. Learning to connect these physical sensations to the emotion is the first, most crucial action step. They are your early warning system, signaling that you must intervene *now*, before the rational brain is fully compromised.

Differentiating Aggression: Reactive vs. Proactive

To effectively calm anger, you must first understand the type of aggression you are struggling with. Social cognition research differentiates between two primary types:

1. **Reactive Aggression:** This is characterized by affective outbursts. It is typically impulsive, driven by a perceived immediate threat, insult, or provocation. Reactive aggression is strongly linked to the cognitive distortion of **misattributing blame to others** and the tendency to **assume the worst** in ambiguous situations. This is the rage that happens when you think someone "did that just to spite me."

2. **Proactive Aggression:** This aggression is more planned, deliberate, and goal-directed. It is often used to achieve a desired outcome, such as bullying for status or manipulating a partner to get your way. This type is linked to self-centered and disagreeable cognitive patterns.

This book primarily focuses on mastering **Reactive Aggression**, as it is the emotional outburst that most often ruins relationships and feels most out of control. The key to mitigating reactive rage is intervening early, focusing on body regulation, and correcting the two primary cognitive distortions that fuel it: blaming others and assuming the worst.

Why Suppression Fails and What to Do Instead

Many people try to manage anger through **suppression**, pushing it down and trying to ignore it. The problem is that suppression is an ineffective, and often damaging, coping mechanism.

Research confirms that while suppression might prevent an immediate external outburst, it is not a significant predictor of overall health or reduced stress. In fact, maladaptive anger inhibition (habitual suppression) is linked to reduced relationship quality and increased physical distress. When you suppress anger, you keep your body in a high-stress state without releasing the energy. The physiological arousal persists, increasing your long-term risk for psychopathology.

The solution is not suppression. It is **regulation** and **expression**.

- **Regulation:** Using physical and cognitive tools to lower the intensity of the feeling (Book 2).

- **Assertive Expression:** Learning to communicate the underlying feeling and need in a clear, respectful way (Book 3).

The next chapters provide a structured path for this regulation, moving from immediate physical techniques to complex cognitive restructuring.

This book moves sequentially, starting with the body, because if the body is calm, the mind can follow, and progresses to the sustained cognitive work necessary for long-term emotional mastery.

1. **Reset Your Body (Chapter 2):** This crucial first step focuses on immediate, physiological intervention. We will teach you the power of controlled breathing, specifically the **4-7-8 breathing protocol**, to directly stimulate the vagus nerve and counteract the fight-or-flight response. You will gain control over your internal state within minutes.

2. **Stop the Cycle (Chapter 3):** We address **anger rumination**, the repetitive, persistent focus on the stressful event that keeps your stress hormones elevated. You will learn actionable interruption techniques to break this destructive cognitive and physiological cycle.

3. **Check Your Story (Chapter 4):** We dismantle the **Hostile Attribution Bias**, the tendency to assume others' actions are malicious. We use cognitive reappraisal techniques to challenge your internal narrative, replacing blame with rational, constructive interpretations.

4. **Think First (Chapter 5):** You will move beyond mere reaction by learning structured **Problem-Solving Skills** to address the actual root cause of your anger. This moves you from feeling like a helpless victim of circumstance to feeling like a competent, solution-oriented agent.

5. **Measure Your Calm (Chapter 6):** We introduce the use of **Heart Rate Variability (HRV)** as an objective index of your progress in emotion regulation. By understanding this measurable, physiological data, you transform anger management from subjective guesswork into a trackable, scientific skill.

The consistent application of these physical and cognitive tools will build emotional resilience, ensuring that calm and thoughtfulness become your new default response to provocation.

The Foundation of Breath: Physical Control Precedes Mental Control

Before we dive into the specific techniques, you must accept one fundamental principle: you cannot reason your way out of a physiological state.

When your heart is racing and your breathing is shallow, your body is convinced you are in danger. No amount of rational thought will override that deeply wired alarm system. Therefore, the first step in anger management must be physiological. You must first use your body to signal safety to your brain.

Your breath is your immediate, non-negotiable tool for intervention. Deep, slow breathing directly reduces physiological arousal and calms the nervous system. This calming effect is mediated by the respiratory vagus nerve. Stimulating this nerve actively counteracts the stress response. The beauty of this intervention is its immediacy and accessibility. You can do it anywhere, instantly, to regain control when the initial physical warnings of anger begin to surface.

The consistency of this practice will be the anchor for every other skill in this book. You need a reliable, rapid tool to achieve that baseline of calm, that low-stress state where your prefrontal cortex can finally resume its job of regulating your emotions and thoughts.

Integrating with Book 1: The Full Circuit

This book is the action-focused counterpart to your cognitive work in Book 1. The skills are deeply interconnected:

- **PFC Restoration:** The cognitive work in *Rewire Your Brain* (Book 1) repaired and strengthened your Prefrontal Cortex (PFC). The physiological regulation skills you learn here in *Calm Anger* (Book 2) are necessary to keep the PFC online and operational when you need it most.

- **Action for Agency:** The commitment to structured action (Chapter 5, Book 1) is reinforced here. The deliberate act of executing a breathing technique or using a problem-solving script is a proactive action that generates a sense of control, which directly counteracts the feelings of helplessness that fuel reactive aggression.

- **Replacing Distortions:** The ability to identify cognitive distortions (Chapter 2, Book 1) is necessary for successfully dismantling the hostile attribution bias (Chapter 4, Book 2). You apply your analytical skill to the specific distortions that arise during conflict.

By systematically addressing the physiological, cognitive, and behavioral aspects of anger, you are building a genuinely resilient and controlled response system. You are taking back control over your most volatile emotional state.

CHAPTER 1

STOP THE BURN:
RESET YOUR BODY THROUGH BREATHING

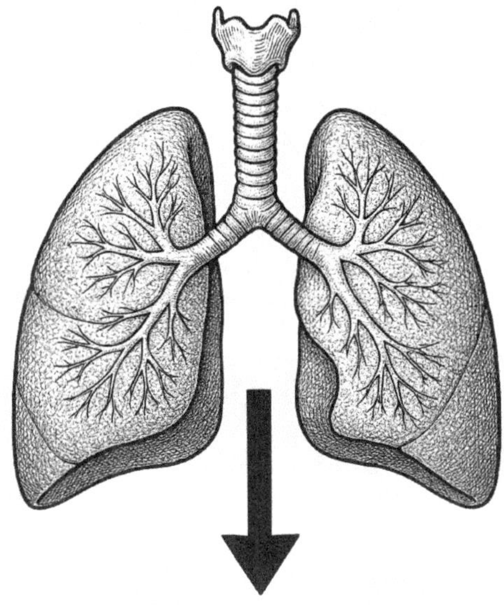

If there was one key takeaway from Book 1, it's that when your body is in panic mode, your emotions have the upper hand. Your logical thinking shuts down as soon as the internal alarm rings. Anger is the strongest of these alarms. When adrenaline and cortisol flood your system, your Prefrontal Cortex, the part of your brain responsible for reason, loses its grip.

Because of this, the first and most effective step in managing anger isn't to debate the angry thought but to calm your body. You must soothe your body's physical reaction before changing your mind's response.

This chapter introduces a powerful tool: controlled breathing. You'll learn a method that activates your body's calming system, overrides the fight-or-flight response, and restores balance in just minutes. This is backed by modern neuroscience, not just theory.

The Immediate Danger:
When Sympathetic Nervous System Takes Over

When anger builds, you notice a racing heart, your face warms, muscles tense, you are experiencing your sympathetic nervous system in overdrive. This is the fight-or-flight mode kicking in. At this point:

- Your heart rate spikes to quickly deliver oxygen to your muscles, readying you for action.

- Your breath becomes shallow and fast, usually held high in your chest, which signals your brain that danger is present.

- Your vagus nerve (the main calming nerve running from brain to body) disengages, removing the natural brake on this alarm state.

Trying to reason with yourself or others in this heightened state is like negotiating with a brain running low on resources. The key is to consciously reactivate the vagus nerve to send a message of safety to your body.

How Controlled Exhalation Works

Breath is unique because, while usually automatic, you can control it consciously. Changing your breath lets you switch your body from panic back to calm.

The secret is in the exhale. A slow, deep exhale stimulates the vagus nerve. This signals your heart and brain that the threat is gone, reducing your physiological stress level in real time. The effect can be tracked by Heart Rate Variability (HRV), which represents the natural variations between heartbeats. When stressed, HRV drops; during calm, it rises. Deep breathing increases HRV, showing your nervous system is stabilizing.

The 4-7-8 Breathing Technique

One of the best methods for quickly calming yourself is the 4-7-8 breathing technique. Rooted in ancient yogic practices called pranayama, it's simple yet powerful for resetting your nervous system. Regular practice sharpens your body's ability to switch modes fast.

Here's how to do it:

1. Preparation: Sit comfortably with an upright posture. Begin by exhaling fully through your mouth, making a soft "whoosh" sound. This clears your lungs and starts the relaxation.

2. Inhale: Close your mouth and breathe in quietly through your nose for a slow count of 4 seconds, filling your belly, not just your chest.

3. Hold: Hold your breath for 7 seconds to allow oxygen to circulate thoroughly.

4. Exhale: Breathe out with a steady "whoosh" sound through your mouth for 8 seconds. This long exhale is what activates your calming system.

5. Repeat: Do this cycle at least 4 times, focusing exclusively on your breath and count to divert attention from angry or anxious thoughts.

Why 4-7-8 Helps

This technique offers both immediate and lasting benefits:

- It reduces anxiety by drawing your focus away from worries and onto breath regulation.
- It supports heart health by improving HRV and lowering blood pressure, especially in younger adults.
- It promotes better sleep by soothing the nervous system and slowing a racing heart.

Using this tool when anger first sparks gives you a physical way to regain control before thoughts take over.

Building Breathwork into Your Anger Awareness

Don't wait until anger overwhelms you to try this, use it as a preventative measure. Start by noticing your body's earliest signs of anger, which indicate sympathetic activation:

Warning Sign	Where It Shows Up	What It Feels Like
Tightening / Clenching	Jaw, fists, shoulders	Tense muscles ready to react
Flushing / Heat	Face, neck, ears	Warmth from rising blood
Shallow Breathing	Chest, stomach	Rapid, shallow breaths
Internal Pressure	Head, chest	Feeling like you might explode

If you spot any of these sensations, immediately start the 4-7-8 breathing cycle. Treat the signal like a fire alarm; don't wait to confirm danger. Stop, breathe, and reset with the controlled exhale.

This approach does two things: it buys you time for your logical brain to come back online and it interrupts the spiral of negative thoughts by shifting focus to breath.

Taking Calm as Your Baseline

Mastering anger control starts by stopping the physical burn early. The 4-7-8 protocol is your go-to tool for instantly engaging your body's own calming system.

This is the foundation for all the strategies the rest of this book will cover. You need this baseline of calm to use later cognitive and communication skills effectively. Make a habit of practicing even when calm, so this calming reflex strengthens. When anger flares, stop the burn. Just breathe. You're reclaiming control of both your body and mind.

CHAPTER 2
DEFUSE THE BOMB:
INTERRUPTING ANGER RUMINATION

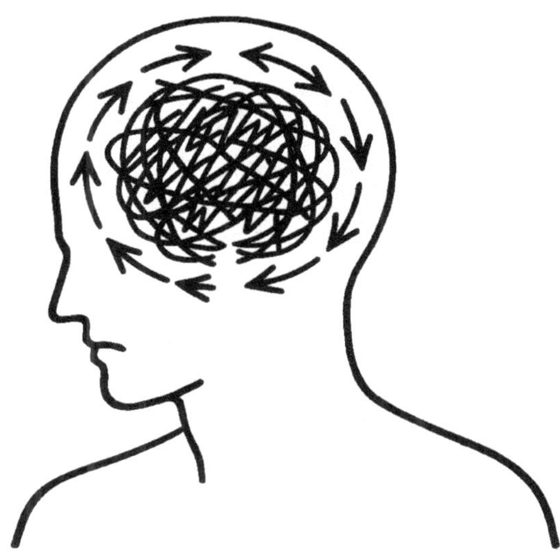

You have established physiological control. When anger's heat begins to rise, you now have the 4-7-8 breathing protocol to force your body out of sympathetic overdrive and restore resources to your rational brain. This ability to *stop the burn* is vital.

But anger often does not stop when the immediate event is over. You may have walked away from the argument or hung up the phone, yet the conversation continues to run on a toxic loop in your mind. You replay the scene, thinking of things you *should* have said, rehearsing future confrontations, or dwelling on the injustice of the situation.

This toxic cycle is called **anger rumination**. It is one of the most damaging psychological habits you can adopt, and it is a major factor in sustaining chronic hostility and stress. This chapter focuses on interrupting that toxic loop, protecting your health, and ensuring that conflict ends when the event ends.

Rumination is defined as the repetitive, persistent focus on the thoughts and feelings related to a stressful or provocative event. It is the mental equivalent of picking at a wound: it prevents healing and ensures the body remains in a heightened state of stress long term.

Research confirms that anger rumination is profoundly detrimental, sustaining negative affective, cognitive, and, critically, **physiological** responses long after the initial stressor has passed.

Here is the measurable damage that rumination causes:

1. **Slower Physiological Recovery:** Studies focusing on stress exposure (such as public speaking tasks) found that rumination predicted a **slower recovery of heart rate** following the stressor. This physiological lag means that instead of returning to an emotional baseline (the rest-and-digest state) minutes after the conflict, your body remains stuck in the high-alert, fight-or-flight state for hours or even days.

2. **Heightened Negative Appraisals:** People who habitually ruminate often generate more negative appraisals of the stressful task *after* it has ended. The thought process convinces you the event was more stressful, threatening, and damaging than it actually was. This creates a cognitive feedback loop where the rumination justifies itself by making the situation seem worse.

3. **Increased Risk for Psychopathology:** Consistent rumination and high levels of perceived stress are significant predictors of heightened anxiety, heightened depression, and decreased overall physical health and well-being. By prolonging the stress response, rumination increases your risk for chronic psychological and physical ailments.

Rumination is a chemical and cognitive commitment to suffering. You cannot afford to let the replay button run unchecked. The only way to mitigate this damage is through actionable interruption.

The Strategy: Cognitive and Behavioral Interruption

When rumination begins, your task is to immediately deploy a structured **diversionary tactic.** This tactic must be powerful enough to physically and mentally shift your focus away from the toxic loop. The interruption must be a planned action, not a passive hope.

We deploy two types of interruption: cognitive and behavioral.

Tool 1: Cognitive Interruption (Thought Replacement)

The moment you catch the loop starting, when you hear the words *should have* or *how dare they*, you must force a mental shift away from the retrospective blame and towards a productive, rational focus.

Action Focus: The Stop-and-Switch

1. **Stop Signal:** Use an immediate, internal signal to halt the loop. This can be a silent, firm word like "Stop," or a visual metaphor, such as imagining a red traffic light or hitting the "pause" button on a remote control. This action acknowledges the thought without fusing with it, echoing the detachment skills you learned in Book 1.

2. **Thought Replacement (Reappraisal):** Once the thought is paused, you must immediately replace it with a predetermined, constructive focus. This uses the principle of **Cognitive Reappraisal**, which is the process of altering the internal narrative to reduce the emotional intensity of a situation.

Instead of letting your mind run wildly, you give it a structured, non-emotional job. This job must be focused on factual reality or problem-solving.

Toxic Rumination Example	Constructive Replacement Focus
"They were deliberately rude just to undermine me. I need to plan a devastating counter-attack."	**Focus on Facts:** "What is the single, non-emotional fact I know about that interaction? *Fact: They stated they would not complete the task until tomorrow.*"
"I should have been faster and more clever. I look like a total idiot."	**Focus on Process:** "What small, specific step can I take right now to solve the remaining problem? *Step: I need to draft three potential solutions for the next meeting.*"
"I am so angry that my heart is racing. This is unbearable."	**Focus on the Breath:** "My job right now is to execute the 4-7-8 protocol until my heart rate slows. I am safe and focused on the count."

By forcing a switch to a factual or self-regulating task, you bypass the emotional circuitry that was driving the rumination. You are using your executive function (PFC) to discipline the limbic system, diverting attention away from the conflict and toward self-control.

Tool 2: Behavioral Interruption (Physical Redirect)

When the rumination is intense and purely cognitive strategies are failing, you must use a **physical redirect**. This involves actively changing your physical state or location to break the loop.

Action Focus: Change the Channel

1. **Physical Activity:** Engaging in physical activity is essential because exercise releases tension and boosts mood-enhancing endorphins, providing a healthy redirect for stored nervous energy. This is not about aggressive exercise; it is about disruption.

   o *Examples:* Go for a ten-minute fast walk, do a set of push-ups, or simply stand up and stretch vigorously. The physical change breaks the mental pattern.

2. **Sensory Grounding:** Engage your five senses to ground yourself firmly in the present moment, pulling your attention away from the internal replay.

   o *Examples:* Touch an object with a distinct texture (a cold glass of water, a rough stone). Focus intensely on the texture, temperature, and weight. Or, intensely observe five specific, small objects in your immediate environment, noting their color and detail.

3. **Scheduled Worry Time:** If the thought persists, make a contract with yourself. You are not suppressing the thought entirely, but postponing it. Tell yourself, "I will not think about this now. I will allocate 15 minutes at 7:00 PM for scheduled worry time." Then, you must commit to that promise. When 7:00 PM arrives, you can review the issue with your TCT and problem-solving skills (Book 1, Chapter 5), but only for the allotted time. This restores control over the thoughts.

The immediate goal is to physically or mentally shift focus to stop the damaging physiological cycle. When the physical body is still, the mind can continue to spin. You must break that stillness.

Successfully interrupting rumination has a direct neuroplastic impact that reinforces the work you did in Book 1.

Every time you choose to stop the toxic loop and deliberately engage a constructive thought (Thought Replacement), you are strengthening the neural pathway associated with self-control and rational engagement.

- **Weakening the Loop:** The old ruminative circuit, where the trigger leads inevitably to repetitive negative thought and sustained stress, weakens through lack of use. The signal along that path becomes less reliable.

- **Strengthening the Regulator:** The new circuit, which links the trigger to the interruption signal and the subsequent constructive focus, is strengthened. This process actively reinforces your PFC's ability to exert reasoned, top-down control over emotional impulses.

Consistency is key. The more you interrupt the pattern, the easier it becomes, until eventually, your brain's default will be to engage a constructive solution rather than fall into the destructive replay.

The Relationship Between Rumination and Cognitive Distortions

Rumination often feeds directly off the cognitive distortions you learned to identify in Book 1. The repetitive loop is rarely based on objective facts; it is usually a continuous restatement of an irrational distortion.

Cognitive Distortion	How It Fuels Rumination	Interruption Strategy
Hostile Attribution	"He didn't include me in the email because he wants me to fail. This is malicious." (Replay focuses on *their* perceived evil intent.)	**Reality Testing (Book 1):** Focus on alternative explanations (e.g., forgetfulness, time pressure).
Should Statements	"I *should* have been perfect. I *shouldn't* have gotten emotional. This is unacceptable." (Replay focuses on impossible standards.)	**Self-Compassion (Book 1):** Replace "should" with "It is acceptable that I am imperfect. I will accept reality and try again."

Cognitive Distortion	How It Fuels Rumination	Interruption Strategy
Catastrophizing	"Because the argument was so intense, the relationship is now certainly ruined forever." (Replay focuses on the predicted terminal consequence.)	**Implications Check (Book 3):** Focus on the realistic consequence: The relationship is stressed, but repair is possible with a planned conversation.

By recognizing the underlying distortion, you can dismiss the entire ruminative chain as invalid. If the core thought is irrational (**Hostile Attribution**), the ensuing 30 minutes of self-torture are also irrational and not worth your time or physiological resources.

Action Plan: Interrupting the Replay

Your commitment is to turn immediate interruption into a reliable habit this week.

Step 1: Identify Your Toxic Script

Listen to your inner voice during rumination. Write down the one or two most common phrases your mind repeats. (e.g., "They will never respect me," or "This whole thing is my fault.")

Step 2: Commit to Immediate Cognitive Interruption

The moment you hear the toxic script begin, immediately deploy the **Stop-and-Switch** technique.

- **Signal:** Say "Stop" silently and firmly.
- **Switch:** Immediately engage in a predetermined, constructive cognitive task. (Example: Force yourself to plan the next two lines of the *Kind Speech* script you will use for repair, or spend 60 seconds listing three good things that happened earlier today.)

Step 3: Use Behavioral Redirect (When Necessary)

If the cognitive switch fails (the loop restarts within 30 seconds), immediately initiate a physical redirect.

- **Action:** Leave the room and perform five minutes of vigorous physical activity (walking, cleaning, stretching).
- **Grounding:** Focus intensely on a sensory detail (the cold of water, the rough texture of a wall) to anchor your mind firmly in the non-ruminating present.

By committing to this action-oriented interruption, you are actively protecting your psychological and physiological health. You are teaching your brain that conflict has a beginning and an end, and that sustained stress is no longer your default response. You are defusing the bomb, and the silence that follows is the sound of your resilience growing.

CHAPTER 3

CHECK YOUR STORY:

DEFEATING THE HOSTILE ATTRIBUTION BIAS

You have learned to calm the raging body using controlled breathing and to interrupt the destructive cycle of rumination. These are essential skills. But the ability to manage anger in the moment means nothing if you continue to operate from a core belief that the world, and the people in it, are actively trying to harm you.

Most reactive anger, the impulsive rage that causes you to lash out or shut down, is not triggered by genuine danger. It is triggered by a **misinterpretation**. You see an ambiguous action and instantly assign the worst possible, most malicious intent to it.

This cognitive distortion is known as the **Hostile Attribution Bias (HAB)**. If someone bumps you in a hallway, your automatic thought is, "They did that on purpose to disrespect me." If a coworker doesn't reply to an email, the story you tell yourself is, "They are deliberately ignoring me to undermine my work." This bias is the fuse that lights the explosive surge of reactive anger.

This chapter teaches you how to systematically check your story against reality. You must dismantle this bias by treating your assumptions about others' intentions as what they are: fearful, irrational predictions that require rigorous, evidence-based testing.

The Anatomy of Hostility: When Perception Becomes Threat

The Hostile Attribution Bias is one of the foundational cognitive distortions fueling reactive aggression. Research on aggression clearly shows that impulsive, affective outbursts are strongly predicted by the tendency to **misattribute blame to others** and to **assume the worst** in ambiguous social situations.

When HAB is active, your mental filter is set to detect malice. Your brain, having just restored some calm using the breathing techniques from Chapter 2, is immediately hijacked by this thought pattern, sending you right back into sympathetic overdrive. The thought creates the threat, and the body reacts accordingly.

The HAB Cycle:

1. **Ambiguous Action:** A coworker offers blunt feedback on your report, stating, "This conclusion is confusing."

2. **Hostile Interpretation (HAB):** Your brain instantly generates the story: "They think I am incompetent. They are trying to embarrass me in front of the team."

3. **Emotional Reaction:** You feel intense anger, humiliation, and a defensive need to fight back or withdraw aggressively.

4. **Reactive Behavior:** You snap back, become rude, or aggressively shut down the conversation.

This cycle is destructive because it is not based on facts. The facts were: "The conclusion is confusing." Your reaction was based entirely on your *interpretation* of the coworker's internal intent, an interpretation you cannot prove. By altering this internal narrative, you can dramatically reduce the emotional intensity of the situation, allowing you to return to an emotional baseline and respond thoughtfully instead of impulsively.

The Core Intervention: Cognitive Reappraisal

The antidote to HAB is **Cognitive Reappraisal**. This is the fundamental process of altering the internal narrative or interpretation of a situation to reduce its emotional intensity. It is the process of checking your story.

Cognitive Reappraisal is a direct action that uses the repaired regulatory power of your PFC (from Book 1) to challenge the emotional interpretation. It involves three quick, structured steps:

1. **Identify the Distorted Thought:** State the HAB assumption clearly. (*"They did that to make me look bad."*)

2. **Challenge the Accuracy:** Systematically question the evidence for that assumption. (*"What facts do I have that prove malicious intent?"*)

3. **Replace with a Constructive Interpretation:** Formulate a balanced, rational alternative. (*"They were likely under stress and spoke too quickly, or they were focused on the task, not my feelings."*)

By consistently altering your internal narrative, you reduce the immediate emotional surge. This allows the person, the thoughtful, problem-solving self, to re-engage, instead of the impulsive, reactive self. The goal is to establish mental space between the ambiguous action and your emotional response.

Action Tool 1: Reality Testing the Intent

The first tool against HAB is **Reality Testing**. You must adopt a scientific, skeptical attitude toward your own mind reading. You cannot afford to react to assumptions. You must react only to verified facts.

Reality Testing requires actively seeking clear, objective evidence to support your negative interpretation. In almost every case, this testing reveals that the extreme assumption is inaccurate or, at the very least, cannot be proven.

The Three Questions of Reality Testing:

When you feel the surge of reactive anger, and you suspect HAB is active, immediately run the scenario through these questions, using the analytical skills you mastered in Book 1 (TCT).

1. What is the Evidence for Malicious Intent?

HAB rests on the assumption that the other person *intended* to cause harm or disrespect you. You must isolate this core assumption and demand proof.

- *Scenario:* A colleague sends an email that severely criticizes your budget proposal, calling it "unrealistic and poorly sourced." Your immediate hostile thought is: "They are trying to destroy my reputation."

- *Reality Test:* List the objective, verifiable facts that *prove* malice.
  - o *Evidence For Malice:* The language was harsh ("unrealistic and poorly sourced"). They did not offer solutions.
  - o *Evidence Against Malice:* The criticism was directed at the *budget*, not your character. The colleague has a reputation for being direct and focused on accuracy. They copied the supervisor, which is standard procedure, not a secret attack. The criticism is fact-based (if the sources were weak).
- *Conclusion:* You find that the evidence for **malicious intent** is weak, while the evidence for **objective criticism** (driven by the coworker's need for accuracy) is strong. The attack was on the *work*, not the *person*.

2. What is the Objective, Neutral Fact?

You must separate the emotional story from the non-negotiable fact. This act of separation immediately reduces the emotional volatility.

- *Hostile Story:* "My partner is refusing to help me because they think their time is more valuable than mine."
- *Objective Fact:* "My partner has not yet helped with the dishes."
- *Hostile Story:* "That driver aggressively cut me off to prove a point."
- *Objective Fact:* "That driver changed lanes quickly in front of me."

By grounding yourself in the neutral fact, you eliminate the emotional heat generated by the assumed hostility. You can now approach the situation (e.g., the dishes or the driving) as a problem to solve, not a personal attack to avenge.

3. What Would a Neutral Observer See?

When you are flooded with anger, your vision is tunnel-like and self-centered. You must force a perspective shift. Imagine a camera recording the event, or ask yourself, "If a kind, neutral stranger watched this interaction, what would they conclude about the other person's *intent*?"

- *Scenario:* You saw a friend fail to wave back at you across a crowded room. Your thought: "They deliberately snubbed me."
- *Neutral Observer Test:* A neutral observer would note: 1) The room was loud and crowded. 2) The friend was mid-conversation, looking at the person they were speaking to. 3) The friend smiled at someone else nearby.

- *Conclusion:* The observer would conclude the friend *did not see you*, or their attention was preoccupied. The story of the "deliberate snub" is a cognitive projection, not a fact.

Consistent use of Reality Testing forces your thoughts out of the emotional limb (the amygdala) and into the rational limb (the PFC), strengthening your capacity for control.

Action Tool 2: Generating Alternative Explanations

The second, non-negotiable step against HAB is the deliberate creation of alternative explanations. HAB relies on binary thinking: either the person is *good* or they are *malicious*. This is a form of All-or-Nothing Thinking, which you learned to fight in Book 1.

You must force your brain to generate multiple, neutral, non-hostile reasons for the ambiguous action. By generating alternatives other than the original, negative, blaming explanation, you broaden your perspective and reduce aggressive behavior.

The Three-Option Rule:

When reacting to an ambiguous action, you must immediately generate three plausible, non-hostile alternative explanations before you are allowed to respond or ruminate.

Ambiguous Action	Initial Hostile Story (HAB)	Three Neutral Alternatives
A colleague submits a task late without warning.	"They are lazy and incompetent, trying to make the rest of us work harder."	1. They are facing a difficult, immediate family emergency.
		2. They misread the deadline or were given conflicting information.
		3. They are struggling with a complex part of the task but are too ashamed to ask for help.
You ask a question, and your supervisor replies with a sigh and	"They are annoyed at me and think my question was stupid."	1. They are extremely stressed from an urgent email they just received.

Ambiguous Action	Initial Hostile Story (HAB)	Three Neutral Alternatives
a short, irritable answer.		2. They did not sleep well last night due to external stress.
		3. They were focused on another project and the interruption broke their concentration.
Your close friend cancels your plan at the last minute with a vague excuse.	"They don't value our friendship and are avoiding me."	1. They feel exhausted and need legitimate solitary downtime (prosocial self-care).
		2. They genuinely forgot another appointment that cropped up.
		3. They are financially strapped and feel embarrassed to admit it.

The simple act of generating these neutral options immediately lowers the emotional temperature. It introduces ambiguity, and ambiguity is the enemy of the hostile attribution bias. If three other explanations are plausible, the hostile story loses its status as *fact* and is downgraded to *speculation*.

The Cognitive Skill of Empathy Training

The long-term solution to defeating HAB is training the cognitive skill of **empathy**. Empathy is the ability to understand and share the feelings of others. It requires cognitive flexibility, which is the ability to attend closely to another person's mental state and generate creative, internally generated responses.

Training empathy directly targets the rigid, black-and-white thinking of HAB. It forces you to consider the contextual and social factors that influence another person's emotional reaction, making it less likely that you will attribute simplified, malicious intentions to them.

Action Focus: Perspective Rehearsal

When someone provokes you, before you respond:

1. **Assume the Best Stressor:** Instead of assuming malice, assume they are reacting to an outside stressor. What is the most plausible, non-hostile reason for their behavior? (*"They are cutting me off because they are running late for an emergency."*)

2. **Generate Their Internal State:** Based on that assumed stressor, try to interpret their internal experience. Are they feeling panic? Fear? Shame? (*"They are likely feeling frantic and out of control, not angry at me."*)

By practicing this perspective rehearsal, you strengthen the neural pathways associated with sophisticated social behavior (the mPFC and dlPFC). This reduces aggressive behavior by providing you with alternative, constructive strategies for responding to perceived threats or conflicts. You replace the automatic, hostile narrative with a nuanced, compassionate hypothesis.

Making Rationality the Default

The work in this chapter, checking your story, reality testing, and practicing empathy, is how you ensure that the skills from Book 1 remain operational when conflict arises. You cannot regulate an emotion that your mind keeps generating through hostile stories.

By moving away from external blame and toward a rigorous internal audit, you stop letting the ambiguous actions of others dictate your emotional state. You seize control of your interpretation, which is the ultimate act of agency in anger management. You are making rationality the default response, preparing yourself for the final, necessary step: structured problem-solving to address the root cause of the conflict, which is the focus of the next chapter.

CHAPTER 4
THINK FIRST: USING PROBLEM-SOLVING SKILLS UNDER STRESS

You have accomplished the immediate work of emotional regulation. You know how to stop the physical surge of rage using controlled breathing, and you know how to stop the toxic internal replay using interruption tactics. Crucially, you learned to check your story, refusing to let the Hostile Attribution Bias trick you into assuming malice.

Now, we face the biggest challenge: what do you do with the regulated calm?

Anger often serves as a distorted signal that a problem exists and you feel powerless to solve it. You get angry because, at a fundamental level, you feel **blocked** and **incompetent** to address the stressor. If you regulate your emotion but fail to address the underlying conflict or unmet need, the frustration simply builds again, eventually overwhelming your hard-won calm. You cannot sustain peace if the conditions that provoke you remain constant.

Effective anger management programs recognize this truth: they do not just focus on suppression or emotional control. They emphasize developing practical, constructive skills to address the very stressors that cause the anger. This chapter teaches you to use **structured problem-solving** as the ultimate, constructive alternative to impulsive aggression. You will learn to move from volatile reaction to thoughtful, planned competence.

The Scientific Case for Competence

Reactive aggression is often associated with failure in **executive function**: specifically, deficits in behavioral inhibition. Aggressive, impulsive behavior is the result of failing to stop, think, and choose a rational response. When you lack a clear plan or skill set to handle a conflict, the easiest and fastest response is often the impulsive, angry one.

Problem-solving skills training directly counteracts this executive function deficit. It provides a structured, learned path that forces you to engage the rational Prefrontal Cortex (PFC), directly replacing impulsive reaction with planned action.

The results are measurable. Structured anger management programs that incorporate problem-solving skills training have been empirically shown to produce significant, positive change.

- **Decreased Anger, Increased Skill:** Studies reveal that participants who undergo this structured training experience a significant decrease in anger levels and, simultaneously, a significant increase in problem-solving skills and communication skills.

- **Competence Over Feeling:** The scores of the experimental groups on problem-solving skills significantly increased after the training program, while the control groups showed no such improvement. This highlights a crucial truth: changing anger is about changing competence, not just changing feelings. You replace the feeling of helplessness with the functional skill of solution-finding.

When you feel capable of solving a problem, the internal alarm that signals "threat" or "helplessness" stops ringing. You move from the passive stance of a victim reacting to circumstance to the active stance of an agent choosing a solution. This is the ultimate act of agency in emotional control.

The 5-Step Structured Problem-Solving Model

To ensure your problem-solving is constructive and not hijacked by residual emotion, you must follow a systematic, step-by-step process. This framework forces clarity, prevents emotional shortcuts, and directs your energy toward resolution.

Step 1: Define the Problem Factually and Specifically

The most common failure in problem-solving is starting with an emotional definition. You cannot solve a feeling. You must define a concrete, actionable problem.

- **Emotional Definition (Unsolvable):** "The problem is that my manager is disrespectful and arrogant." (This is a judgment, not a problem.)
- **Factual Definition (Solvable):** "The problem is that my manager assigns me tasks through text messages after 8:00 PM, infringing on my personal time and causing stress." (This is a specific, measurable behavior.)

You must use the skills from Book 1 (TCT) to strip the emotion away and reduce the issue to its objective, neutral facts. If the problem is still vague, like "I feel overwhelmed", you must ask yourself: *What specific circumstance, conversation, or task is causing the overwhelmed feeling?* The problem definition must be **Specific** and **Measurable** (the "SM" in the SMART goal framework).

Action Commitment (Step 1):

- **Avoid "Why":** Avoid asking, "Why am I angry?" This encourages rumination and blame.
- **Focus on "What":** Ask, "What specific behavior, event, or lack of resource is creating this difficulty?"
- **Identify the Gap:** Define the discrepancy between the current reality and your desired outcome.

This clarity ensures your problem-solving efforts target the root cause, not the emotional symptom.

Step 2: Generate Solutions Without Judgment (Brainstorming)

Once the problem is defined factually, the next step is to generate a wide range of potential solutions. Critically, during this brainstorming phase, you must adopt a rule of **zero judgment**.

The natural impulse, especially when feeling insecure or angry, is to immediately shoot down ideas: "That's stupid," "That won't work," or "I could never do that." This judgment is the voice of the inner critic (Book 1) and the fear of failure (Learned Helplessness). It prematurely shuts down creativity.

Action Commitment (Step 2):

- **Quantity Over Quality:** Set a target to generate at least five to ten distinct potential solutions, no matter how unrealistic they may seem initially. Write down every idea.

- **Include Extremes:** Include both highly aggressive solutions (e.g., "Quit my job immediately") and highly passive solutions (e.g., "Do nothing and hope it goes away"). This helps to anchor the range of possibilities and makes the rational middle ground easier to see later.

- **Focus on Self-Action:** Ensure at least half the solutions focus on actions *you* can take to change your behavior or environment, rather than relying on others to change theirs.

This generative phase is crucial because it immediately combats the learned helplessness state by proving to your brain that **you have options**. The abundance of options restores the dopamine flow associated with agency, reinforcing the motivation to act.

Step 3: Evaluate Consequences (Cost-Benefit Analysis)

Now, you apply cold, hard reason. You take the list of ten solutions and subject each one to a realistic, impartial cost-benefit analysis. This step prevents you from impulsively choosing the most emotionally satisfying but ultimately destructive solution (e.g., lashing out).

Action Commitment (Step 3):

For each potential solution, ask two sets of questions:

1. **Short-Term Impact (Costs):** What are the immediate negative consequences of this action? (Will it cause more conflict? Will it cost money? Will it create more work?)

2. **Long-Term Impact (Rewards):** What are the ultimate positive outcomes of this action, and how well does it align with my core values (e.g., integrity, peace, health)? (Will this solve the problem permanently? Will I feel respected? Will it prevent future anger?)

This evaluation forces a time perspective. Reactive anger is focused only on the immediate release of tension (a short-term reward). Problem-solving forces you to prioritize long-term, sustainable rewards, which is a hallmark of strong executive function and emotional maturity.

Step 4: Choose the Best Action and Plan Implementation

Based on your evaluation in Step 3, select the solution that maximizes long-term positive rewards while minimizing realistic short-term costs. Once chosen, the action must be defined clearly within the SMART framework to ensure completion.

Action Commitment (Step 4):

- **The Choice:** Select the most effective, constructive, and **Attainable** solution. (Example: "I will use the DESC script to assert a time boundary with my manager.")

- **Implementation Plan (SMART):** Define the step:
    - *Action:* I will send the boundary-setting email.
    - *Time-based:* I will write the draft by 10:00 AM tomorrow and send it at 2:00 PM.
    - *Measurable:* The success is sending the email, regardless of the immediate response. (You separate the action from the outcome.)

By focusing on the process, the *sending* of the email, rather than the outcome, the *manager's feeling*, you retain control and ensure a guaranteed win, which is essential for reinforcing agency.

Step 5: Implement and Review (Adaptation)

The final step is to execute the plan and then review its effectiveness honestly. You must measure the result against your initial goal, not against a standard of perfection.

- *Review Question 1:* Did the action solve the problem as defined in Step 1?

- *Review Question 2:* What were the unexpected costs or rewards?

- *Review Question 3:* If it did not fully solve the problem, what is the next small, measurable action I can take (return to Step 2)?

This final review closes the loop, transforming any necessary failure into a data point for learning, rather than a reason for aggressive self-blame. This adaptive approach replaces the rigidity of the inner critic with the flexibility of a scientist.

The Role of Emotional Regulation in Problem-Solving

You cannot execute this 5-step model while feeling intense anger. The cognitive resources required for Step 3 (Evaluation) and Step 2 (Non-judgmental Brainstorming) are simply unavailable when the amygdala is running the show.

This is where the integration with Chapter 2 becomes non-negotiable.

Action Sequence Under Stress:

1. **Trigger Event Occurs (e.g., The manager texts after 8 PM).**
2. **Physical Cue Arises (The Burn):** You feel the heart rate spike, the jaw clench, the heat rise.
3. **Immediate Interruption (Chapter 2):** Stop everything. Execute the 4-7-8 breathing protocol until the heart rate slows and the physical tension decreases. You must achieve a baseline state of calm.
4. **Cognitive Audit (Chapter 4):** While calm, quickly check your story. Is this **Hostile Attribution Bias**? What are three non-malicious reasons for the text? (Example: "They are disorganized, not malicious.")
5. **Problem-Solving Initiation (Chapter 5):** Only once the initial emotional heat is gone, you can safely engage Step 1: "What is the factual problem that needs solving?"

By integrating the physiological calm (breath) and the cognitive audit (checking the story) *before* engaging problem-solving, you ensure that the solution is constructive, not reactive. This structured response system is the hallmark of resilient emotional health. It provides a highly effective alternative strategy for responding to perceived threats or conflicts, which is proven to reduce aggressive behavior.

Problem-Solving for Aggression and Executive Function

Problem-solving directly addresses the neurocognitive deficits associated with reactive aggression. Aggressive, impulsive behavior is often linked to poor **behavioral inhibition** and frontal lobe dysfunction.

When you feel provoked, your impulse is to yell, slam a door, or send an angry text. This is an inhibition failure. The 5-step problem-solving process is a deliberate, highly structured inhibition drill.

- **Inhibition:** By forcing yourself to pause (Step 1) and generate multiple, non-judgmental options (Step 2), you inhibit the immediate aggressive impulse.

- **Executive Control:** By forcing a rational cost-benefit analysis (Step 3), you engage your PFC in a high-level cognitive task, pulling resources away from the emotional limbic system.

This intentional engagement of the PFC, choosing the hard, rational path over the easy, emotional one, strengthens your neural ability to maintain control in all future conflicts. You are replacing the aggression circuit with a competence circuit.

The Default of Competence

You have learned that controlling anger is not about superhuman willpower. It is about having a superior set of skills and a reliable sequence of actions. You can calm your body, interrupt the destructive replay, and prevent hostile interpretations.

This chapter completes the practical toolkit by giving you the final skill: structured competence. By consistently applying the 5-step problem-solving model under stress, you transform the feeling of helplessness into one of genuine empowerment and control. You are ensuring that when conflict inevitably arises, your default response is not rage, but thoughtful action. This resilience, the ability to act constructively when provoked, is the ultimate sign that you have taken back control. The next chapter will provide you with the objective data to prove that this internal shift is happening.

CHAPTER 5

MEASURE YOUR CALM:
USING HRV TO TRACK REGULATION PROGRESS

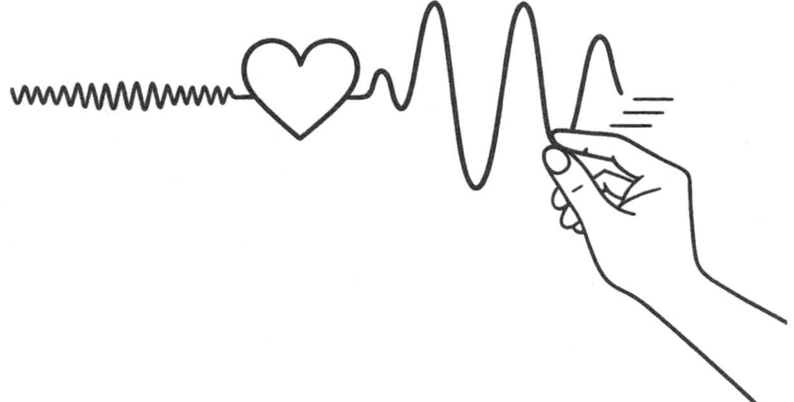

You have successfully built an action-oriented system for handling anger. You have physical tools (controlled breathing) to stop the immediate physiological surge, cognitive tools (reappraisal) to prevent the surge from restarting, and behavioral tools (problem-solving) to address the root cause of the frustration.

The critical question now is: How do you know if it is working?

Emotional change often feels subjective. You might feel calmer today, only to worry tomorrow that the old anger will return. To build lasting confidence in your resilience, you need objective, measurable proof that your internal systems are strengthening. You need a way to move anger management from subjective effort to trackable, scientific skill.

This proof exists in your own body: **Heart Rate Variability (HRV)**. HRV is a precise, physiological index of how well your body and brain regulate internal stress. By learning to measure and influence your HRV, you gain an objective metric of your progress in emotional control, ensuring that calm becomes a verifiable, resilient state.

Heart Rate Variability (HRV) is not the measure of your heart rate itself. It is the measure of the healthy, desirable fluctuation in the time interval between successive heartbeats. Your heart rate is not perfectly metronomic; it naturally speeds up slightly when you inhale and slows down slightly when you exhale. This fluctuation is a good thing.

HRV is often referred to as an index of the balance between your two key nervous systems:

1. **Sympathetic Nervous System (The Accelerator):** Activated by stress, fear, or anger. When this system dominates, the heartbeat becomes rigid, uniform, and fast. This results in **low HRV**.

2. **Parasympathetic Nervous System (The Brake):** Activated by relaxation and calm, primarily through the vagus nerve. When this system dominates, the heart rate exhibits greater, healthier fluctuations. This results in **high HRV**.

A higher, healthier HRV indicates stronger vagus nerve function, improved overall health, and, critically, **improved emotion regulation capacity**. When you are highly reactive, stressed, or experiencing chronic anger, your HRV drops low, signaling that your brake pedal (the parasympathetic system) is disengaged. When you successfully calm yourself using the techniques from this book, your HRV should rise immediately. This objective data proves your intervention worked.

HRV Biofeedback: Training Your Internal Brake

HRV biofeedback training uses technology (often a small sensor worn on a finger or chest) to give you real-time visual or auditory feedback on your HRV levels. This allows you to literally see the impact of your breathing and mental focus on your internal state.

The technology measures your current HRV and guides you to breathe at your optimal pace: the rate that maximizes the fluctuation between heartbeats. For most people, this optimal pace is around 6 breaths per minute (a slow inhale and a slower exhale).

How Biofeedback Works:

1. **Real-Time Data:** You watch a monitor that graphically displays your HRV. When you breathe quickly or hold tension, the line is jagged and low.

2. **Guided Practice:** You are guided to slow your breath, focusing particularly on the long, controlled exhale (the key to vagus nerve stimulation, as discussed in Chapter 2).

3. **Visible Success:** As you hit the optimal pace, the graph or sound signal instantly changes, showing a large, smooth wave of fluctuation (high HRV). This provides tangible, immediate proof that your conscious effort is physically changing your internal state.

The measurable results of this training are compelling and support its use as a tool for anger management:

- **Increased Vagal Tone:** Studies show that training using biofeedback leads to higher HRV during anger induction compared to control groups. This means participants who trained with biofeedback were physically more resilient to the physiological spike caused by provocation.

- **Reduced Anger Intensity:** Furthermore, studies combining HRV biofeedback with structured cognitive-behavioral strategies have shown a **significant decrease in both the intensity and frequency of anger episodes**. These improvements were often maintained for six months following the intervention, demonstrating a lasting shift in emotional resilience.

Using HRV biofeedback shifts anger management from a vague promise to a quantifiable, self-monitored skill. It provides the objective validation you need to build confidence in your ability to maintain calm, even when provoked.

Practical Application: Self-Monitoring Without a Machine

Even without dedicated biofeedback equipment, you can use the *principles* of HRV monitoring to improve your self-awareness and track your regulation progress. The concept is called **Subjective-Objective Correlation.**

You pair your internal, subjective feeling of stress with an objective, measurable physical response you can track.

Action Tool 1: The Three-Minute Baseline Check

You must learn to check your physiological state before and after an intervention.

1. **Baseline Measurement:** When you are calm (such as first thing in the morning or after a 4-7-8 session), count your resting heart rate by placing two fingers on your wrist or neck. Count the beats in 15 seconds and multiply by four to get beats per minute (BPM). Note the quality of your breathing: slow, deep, or shallow? This is your *calm baseline.*

2. **Anger Induction Check:** The moment you feel the physical warning signs of anger, the "burn" described in Chapter 2, immediately pause. Before you act, take a rapid 15-second count of your heart rate and check your breath quality. This confirms that your body is in sympathetic overdrive.

3. **Intervention and Re-Check:** Immediately execute four cycles of the 4-7-8 breathing protocol. After the fourth cycle, re-check your heart rate and breath quality.

The Goal: You should see a measurable drop in BPM (Objective) and a noticeable shift in breath quality (Subjective). The objective evidence (lower BPM) confirms that your intervention (4-7-8) successfully stimulated the vagus nerve and counteracted the fight-or-flight response. This physical, measurable success reinforces your belief in the technique.

Action Tool 2: Tracking the Vagal Brake

You can track your increasing resilience by monitoring two key physiological indicators that rely on the vagus nerve:

1. **Recovery Time (The Bounce-Back):** How long does it take for your heart rate and breathing to return to your *calm baseline* after a stressful event or argument? When you start this practice, recovery might take 20–30 minutes. As your resilience and HRV improve, your recovery time should steadily decrease to 5–10 minutes. Tracking this metric confirms you are successfully interrupting rumination (Chapter 3) and restoring physiological balance faster.

2. **Trigger Tolerance (The Peak Heart Rate):** As your regulatory system strengthens, you should notice that the same old triggers (e.g., traffic, a rude colleague) no longer cause the dramatic spike in heart rate they once did. The anger might register, but the *intensity* (the highest BPM achieved) should be lower. This indicates that your vagal brake is stronger and engages faster.

HRV training is fundamentally about improving your body's ability to maintain dynamic equilibrium, its capacity to adapt and recover from stress. By treating your heart rate and breath as objective data points, you gain confidence that your internal systems are repairing.

The measurable calm generated by HRV-focused techniques is the critical bridge between the body and the mind. When your HRV is high, your PFC is operational, making the complex cognitive work from Book 1 and the problem-solving skills from Chapter 5 of Book 2 possible.

- **Enabling Cognitive Reappraisal:** It is impossible to generate the required three neutral, non-hostile alternative explanations (Chapter 4) when your body is pumping adrenaline. You must first use breath to lower the physiological arousal (increase HRV). The subsequent calm *enables* your PFC to access the memory, logic, and cognitive flexibility needed for successful reappraisal.

- **Supporting Problem-Solving:** Structured problem-solving (Chapter 5) requires rational assessment of consequences and creative generation of solutions. This high-level thinking is a PFC function. By ensuring your body is in a regulated state (high HRV) before attempting problem definition, you guarantee that your solutions are constructive, not impulsive.

The combination of biofeedback, even self-monitored biofeedback, with cognitive-behavioral strategies results in the most sustainable decrease in the frequency and intensity of anger episodes. You are not just learning a trick; you are fundamentally changing the operating parameters of your nervous system.

Trusting the Objective Data

The work in this book has been dedicated to empowering you with control. You now possess the tools to stop the physical burn (Chapter 2), stop the mental replay (Chapter 3), and stop the hostile narrative (Chapter 4).

Chapter 6 provides the verification. By understanding and tracking your Heart Rate Variability, even through simple self-monitoring, you transition from hoping for change to proving it. The objective, measurable data of your own heart rate confirms that your deliberate actions are physically building resilience and increasing your capacity for emotional regulation.

This confidence, built on verifiable evidence, ensures that you can trust your calm. You are no longer vulnerable to unpredictable surges of rage. You are ready for the final step: cementing this controlled response as your reliable, default state.

CONCLUSION

BUILDING RESILIENCE:
MAKING CALM YOUR DEFAULT RESPONSE

You have completed the essential work of taking back control. This book, *Take Back Control*, moved you from a state of impulsive reaction, where anger was a physiological hijacking, to a state of measured, thoughtful response. You proved that anger is manageable, not inevitable. It is not an uncontrollable force of nature, but a predictable, reversible set of physical and cognitive responses.

The transition achieved here is profound. You moved from externalizing blame, believing others were responsible for your feelings, to accepting internal control. By focusing on your body, your thoughts, and your competence, you established a new system where calm is not a lucky accident. It is your reliable, default state.

Let us review the integrated sequence of actions you have mastered, confirming how each skill structurally reinforces the others to build genuine emotional resilience.

The effectiveness of this system lies in its unwavering commitment to action, starting with the physical and moving sequentially to the cognitive.

1. The Physiological Override: Restoring the Brake

You recognized that you cannot reason with a body convinced it is in danger. Therefore, the first step in control is physical.

- **The Action:** You mastered the **4-7-8 breathing protocol** and the principle of the controlled exhale. The moment you detect the physiological warning signs of anger, the "burn", you initiate this technique immediately.

- **The Neuroscientific Effect:** The long, controlled exhale actively stimulates the respiratory vagus nerve, which is the main component of your parasympathetic nervous system (the "brake"). This action overrides the fight-or-flight response, lowers physiological arousal, and, critically, restores blood flow and resources to your Prefrontal Cortex (PFC). This intervention is the non-negotiable step that gives your rational mind the time and resources it needs to function.

By consistently applying this tool, you strengthen the physical capacity for emotion regulation. This is visibly confirmed by increased Heart Rate Variability (HRV), which is the objective metric proving your vagal brake is stronger and engages faster.

2. The Cognitive Firewall: Stopping the Leak

With the body regulated, you addressed the mental patterns that previously caused anger to persist and return.

- **The Action (Chapter 3):** You learned to interrupt **anger rumination**, the repetitive, toxic replay of conflict, using structured cognitive and behavioral diversionary tactics. By employing the **Stop-and-Switch** technique, you broke the damaging loop that sustains high-stress hormones long after the event has passed. This protects your health and accelerates your physiological recovery time.

- **The Action (Chapter 4):** You learned to check your story by dismantling the **Hostile Attribution Bias (HAB)**. You used **Reality Testing** and the **Three-Option Rule** to prove that your assumptions of others' malice were often irrational projections, not facts.

- **The Neuroplastic Effect:** This cognitive work directly reduces the triggers that cause your amygdala (alarm bell) to fire, strengthening the control exerted by your PFC. You replace the rigid, blaming thought patterns that fuel reactive aggression with flexible, reality-based hypotheses. This is how you stop letting the ambiguous actions of others dictate your emotional state.

3. The Competence Circuit: Replacing Helplessness with Agency

The final, essential step was moving beyond mere emotional control to functional, constructive engagement with the stressor.

- **The Action:** You committed to the **5-Step Structured Problem-Solving Model**. This framework forces you to define the problem factually, generate non-judgmental options, and select the solution that maximizes long-term gain over short-term impulsive release.

- **The Neuroscientific Effect:** This structured engagement of high-level cognitive function strengthens executive function and **behavioral inhibition**, deficits often associated with aggressive behavior. By consistently choosing the hard, rational path of problem-solving (Chapter 5) over the easy, emotional path of aggression, you strengthen the neural circuit for competence. This measurable shift directly counteracts the feeling of **learned helplessness** by repeatedly affirming that your effort *can* produce positive, measurable results.

The results of this integrated approach are sustained and measurable: Anger management programs focused on problem-solving demonstrate a significant decrease in anger levels and a corresponding increase in problem-solving skills, leading to better overall adjustment when compared to control groups. You are not just learning to feel calmer; you are learning to be **functionally more competent**.

The Commitment to Resilience

Resilience is not the absence of stress or anger. It is the efficiency and speed with which you can execute this intervention sequence when provocation occurs. Your goal is to make this structured response, Calm Body, Check Story, Find Solution, an automatic reflex.

Your continued success relies on two non-negotiable principles:

1. **Objective Verification:** You must continue to monitor your physiological data. Tracking your Heart Rate and Recovery Time (Chapter 6) provides the empirical evidence that your resilience is increasing. When you see your heart rate return to baseline faster after an argument, you gain confidence that your system is repaired, making it easier to trust your new, calm default.

2. **Repetition and Practice:** Neuroplastic change requires repetition. Every time you successfully execute the 4-7-8 breathing protocol, you reinforce the vagal brake. Every time you consciously generate three alternative explanations for a hostile thought, you weaken the Hostile Attribution Bias. The sustained application of these action tools ensures that the positive changes you have wrought in your body and mind become durable traits, not temporary states.

The next challenge lies in how you use this profound internal calm to engage with others. Volatile anger is rooted in poor communication, a failure to express needs clearly and assertively. The foundation of calm you have built here is the absolute prerequisite for the successful communication strategies you will learn in Book 3.

You have taken back control of your internal world. Now, let us learn how to speak with kindness and power.

REFLECTION QUESTIONS

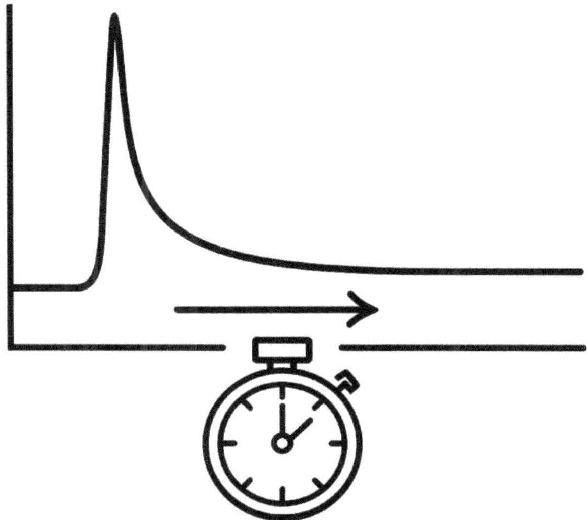

1. Describe the physiological warning signs (e.g., in your jaw, chest, or breathing) you now recognize before anger escalates. How often this week did you successfully initiate the 4-7-8 breathing protocol during this *early* stage?

2. What is the highest Heart Rate (BPM) you measured during a moment of stress this week, and how long did it take for your heart rate and breathing to return to your *calm baseline* after you performed the 4-7-8 breathing technique?

3. Describe a moment this week where you experienced anger rumination. What specific interruption strategy (e.g., physical redirect, **Stop-and-Switch**) did you use to break the cycle, and how quickly did the ruminative loop halt?

4. Identify the most common ambiguous action that triggers your Hostile Attribution Bias (e.g., a delayed email, a blank stare). What were three non-hostile, realistic alternative explanations you generated to neutralize that thought this week?

5. Describe a recent conflict or frustration that you addressed using the **5-Step Problem-Solving Model**. What was the specific, measurable action (Step 4) you chose, and how did executing that action replace the feeling of helplessness with a sense of competence?

BOOK THREE

CONNECT CLEARLY:
ACTIONABLE MODELS FOR KIND SPEECH

INTRODUCTION

THE IMPACT OF WORDS:
WHY HURTFUL SPEECH CAUSES DAMAGE

You have secured your internal life. You can now calm your body when provoked (Book 2) and control your thoughts when challenged (Book 1). That resilience is the highest form of self-respect. Now, we turn outward.

The greatest challenge for a person leaving behind rude or hurtful habits is communication. The words you use, and how you use them, are the primary instruments for building, maintaining, or destroying relationships. A simple argument, poorly phrased, can override months of careful internal work. You can be calm internally, yet your words can still cause immense damage, leading to conflict, isolation, and regret.

Hurtful speech and chronic rudeness represent a fundamental breakdown in **prosocial behavior**, the actions intended to help others and characterized by concern for their feelings and welfare. When you engage in verbal aggression, you erode the very fabric of social connection. Conversely, learning kind, clear, and assertive speech is vital because it is the mechanism by which you forge trust, articulate your needs, and uphold your dignity without resorting to anger.

Hurtful habits are not only destructive to the recipient; they are detrimental to the speaker's well-being. Prosocial behaviors, simple acts of kindness, like holding a door or offering clear support, provide measurable benefits for the person offering the help. Research shows that people who frequently engage in prosocial actions are more likely to experience better moods and, critically, tend to experience negative moods less frequently. Kindness is a natural stress detox.

Hostile communication, however, prevents these benefits and introduces significant relationship costs:

1. **The Intent vs. Perception Gap:** Rudeness is often a function of miscommunication, where the speaker's intent does not match the listener's perception. Every conversation, in effect, involves three dynamics: What was said, what was meant, and what was heard. A direct communicator, for instance, might say exactly what they mean without hedging, aiming for clarity. But this bluntness can be perceived by the listener as harshness or rudeness, especially when social grace is lacking. The speaker's desire for clarity is lost, and the listener receives only the damage.

2. **Defensiveness and Alienation:** Language that relies on moralistic evaluation, judgment, demands, or blame is guaranteed to make the listener defensive. When people feel accused ("You always do that," "You are the problem"), they stop listening and immediately move to protect themselves. This defensiveness prevents the honest addressing of the underlying problem, leading to unresolved conflict and alienation.

3. **Social Exchange Failure:** From the perspective of Social Exchange Theory (SET), all relationships are sustained by balancing rewards against costs. Respect, validation, and kindness are high rewards. Rudeness, judgment, and emotional dumping are high costs. When your communication style consistently imposes high emotional costs on others, the relationship is judged as inequitable and often diminished or ended. Spreading respect, therefore, is about communicating in a way that establishes you as a high-value partner in social exchange.

To move past these damaging patterns, you need a precise, structured language that minimizes friction and ensures your message, your true need, is delivered and received with mutual respect. You need models for clear, compassionate communication.

Most people grew up speaking a language that encourages labeling, comparing, demanding, and pronouncing moral judgments, rather than being aware of what we are genuinely feeling and needing. This judgmental language is insidious and pervasive. It is why conflict escalates so quickly.

When you say, "You are so lazy for leaving the dishes out," you are not describing a fact; you are attaching a global, negative **label** (a cognitive distortion from Book 1) to a person based on a single behavior. The listener does not hear your frustration about the dirty kitchen. They hear, "I judge your core worth as deficient," and they react accordingly.

This language, the language of comparison, blame, and moralistic evaluation, is what we must replace. The objective is to shift your communication from expressing *judgment* about the other person to expressing your *feelings and needs* related to their actions. This fundamental shift is what builds connection instead of conflict.

The Four-Part Action Plan for Clear Connection

The remaining chapters provide the structured, actionable models needed to master clear, kind speech. This plan moves you from recognizing the damage of hostile language to implementing practical, assertive communication frameworks.

1. **Use the Need-Based Language (Chapter 2):** You will learn and implement the **Four Steps of Nonviolent Communication (NVC)**, moving away from judgments and toward articulating observations, feelings, needs, and specific requests. This builds a foundation of mutual trust and connection, preventing conflicts before they start.

2. **Speak with Power (Chapter 3):** You will master **Assertiveness** as a core communication skill, learning to stand up for your rights and express your needs directly and honestly while respecting the rights of others. We introduce the **DESC Script** as a precise, four-step framework for managing difficult conversations and setting clear expectations.

3. **Engage the Other (Chapter 4):** You will train the cognitive skill of **Empathy**, the ability to understand the feelings of others, which is essential for nuanced social interaction and requires cognitive flexibility in the brain. This skill helps you accurately interpret the contextual factors of a conversation.

4. **Connect with Self and Others (Chapter 5, 6):** You will learn techniques to move past internal judgment toward **Compassion,** and you will master the difficult, final step: **repairing conflict** using kind, accountable dialogue.

The foundation for this work is the internal calm you cultivated in Book 2. You must achieve physiological regulation before attempting these high-stakes conversations. Now, with your body calm and your mind clear, you can take control of your words.

The Scientific Imperative: Why Structured Communication Works

Communication models like Nonviolent Communication (NVC) and the DESC script are not just subjective tools; they are structured frameworks that force the brain to engage its regulatory circuits and improve social cognition.

- **Increased Empathy:** Research shows that NVC training increases empathy and successfully reduces interpersonal tension and conflict. Even brief training can lead to improved empathy months later, demonstrating the lasting cognitive impact of this structured approach. By forcing you to articulate the other person's *feelings* and *needs*, NVC strengthens the neural pathways in your prefrontal cortex linked to social cognition.

- **Reduced Defensiveness:** Assertive models, particularly the DESC script, significantly decrease defensiveness in the listener. This occurs because you are trained to use "I" statements to express your feelings and needs, rather than "You" statements, which trigger blame and defensive reactions. By making the conversation about your internal state, you invite collaboration instead of resistance.

- **Stress Reduction:** Assertiveness itself is a proven coping skill that reduces stress and anger. By standing up for your interests directly and respectfully, you eliminate the buildup of resentment that often fuels chronic frustration. When you respect yourself enough to set boundaries and state your needs, your body registers lower stress levels.

The move toward clear, kind, and assertive speech is an act of self-respect that generates social rewards for everyone involved. It guarantees you the best chance of successful communication because the direct, respectful delivery ensures the message is heard, not lost in an aggressive or passive delivery style.

CHAPTER 1

SAY WHAT YOU MEAN:
THE 4 STEPS OF NONVIOLENT COMMUNICATION

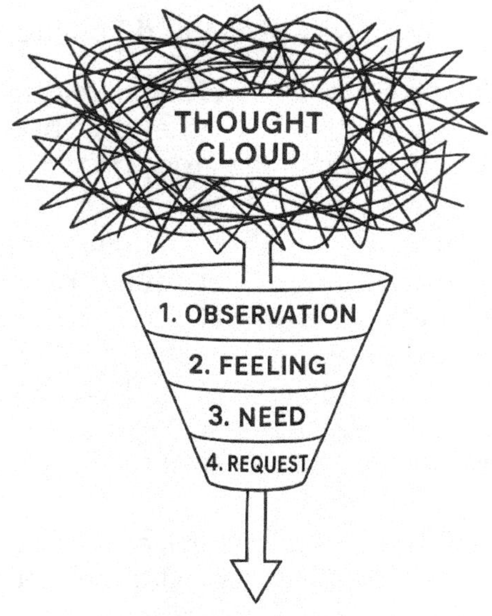

You have mastered the hardest part: achieving internal calm (Book 2). You can regulate the surge, stop the toxic replay, and check your assumptions about malice. You are now internally prepared to engage in high-stakes conversations without letting emotion hijack your response.

However, internal control is only half the battle. When you open your mouth, you face the persistent risk of falling back into the default language of conflict. Most people, even when calm, speak a language rooted in judgment, blame, and demands. This language, as we established, makes the listener defensive, causing the conversation to fail instantly, regardless of your good intentions.

This chapter provides the critical linguistic structure to ensure your words build connection and clarity instead of conflict. You will learn the **Four Steps of Nonviolent Communication (NVC)**, a framework developed by psychologist Marshall Rosenberg. NVC is not about being passive or nice; it is a radically clear and assertive method for expressing yourself and hearing others through the lens of shared human needs, bypassing judgment and reducing friction. This structured language is the foundation for genuine, kind speech.

The Scientific Necessity of Needs-Based Language

NVC is fundamentally based on a scientific hypothesis: all human behavior is an attempt to meet universal human needs (e.g., safety, understanding, connection, autonomy). When needs are met, we feel pleasant emotions (joy, contentment). When needs are unmet, we feel unpleasant emotions (frustration, anger, sadness).

The problem with conventional language is that when our needs are unmet, we express this through blame and judgment: "I am frustrated because *you* are so irresponsible." This statement attacks the other person's character, guaranteeing defensiveness and stopping any productive conversation.

NVC works by training individuals to translate these destructive judgments into factual observations and articulated needs. This structured approach accomplishes three critical goals that promote prosocial behavior:

1. **Reduces Defensiveness:** By using "I" statements and focusing on observable actions rather than inherent character flaws, NVC lowers the listener's immediate emotional reaction. The listener is invited to collaborate rather than resist.

2. **Increases Empathy:** The framework forces both parties to look for the universal human need beneath the surface emotion. By identifying the shared need (e.g., *I need connection*, *You need respect*), empathy is automatically fostered, which reduces interpersonal tension.

3. **Builds Mutual Trust:** Consistent use of NVC, even in brief training sessions, has been shown to increase empathy and reduce interpersonal tension and conflict. This practice builds a durable foundation of mutual trust and respect in day-to-day communication, preventing minor friction from escalating into major conflicts.

NVC is often referred to as preparation for the biggest conflict of your life, because it trains you to act with trust and respect when you are about to say the insult that could ruin a relationship forever.

NVC requires strict adherence to four sequential steps. These steps move you logically from the objective facts of the situation to a clear, actionable request.

Step 1: Observation (Just the Facts, No Judgment)

The first step requires describing the concrete actions or words seen or heard, without adding any evaluation, judgment, or comparison. This is the hardest step for most people, because conventional language fuses observation and judgment instantly.

- **Problematic Judgment:** "You never listen to me." (This is a generalization and a label.)

- **Neutral Observation:** "I noticed that when I was talking about the meeting just now, you looked down at your phone for thirty seconds." (This is a verifiable, objective fact.)

The goal is to provide a clear, neutral piece of data that the other person cannot easily dispute. If the observation contains judgment, the conversation ends before it begins, because the listener immediately shifts into justifying or defending their character. You must stick to what a neutral camera would record.

Step 2: Feelings (Share Pure Emotion, Not Blame)

The second step is to share the genuine emotional response to the observation. You must use "pure feeling words", words that describe your internal state (e.g., sad, happy, frustrated, confused), rather than "blame words", words that imply the other person caused your state (e.g., rejected, manipulated, ignored).

- **Blame Word (Masked Judgment):** "I feel *ignored* when you look at your phone." (The word "ignored" is a judgment that assigns malicious intent to the other person.)

- **Pure Feeling Word:** "I felt **hurt** and **frustrated** when I saw you looking at your phone." (Hurt and frustrated are genuine internal states.)

Using "I feel" statements is critical here. Assertive communication (which NVC supports) requires you to express your thoughts and feelings directly using "I" statements, which avoids putting the listener on the defensive, ensuring they are more likely to listen. This step builds empathy by opening up your emotional world to the listener.

Step 3: Needs (Express the Universal Human Requirement)

This is the most transformative step. You must articulate the universal human need that lies beneath the feeling. This is the **source** of your emotion. Needs are basic human requirements shared by everyone, such as respect, safety, understanding, connection, or autonomy.

- **Initial Thought:** "I felt hurt."
- **Underlying Need:** "I need to feel **heard** and **valued** when we talk."

Stating the need is crucial for two reasons:

1. **It Builds Empathy:** It shows the listener that your reaction is not arbitrary; it is rooted in a fundamental human requirement that *they also share.* This fosters immediate connection and collaboration.

2. **It Defuses Conflict:** Once the core need is identified, the conversation shifts from debating the phone usage to collaborating on meeting the need for "being valued." This is a problem you can solve together. We are often not taught to think in terms of needs, but mastering this translation is the key to lucidity in interpersonal relationships.

Step 4: Request (Make a Clear, Specific, Actionable Invitation)

The final step is to make a clear, specific, and actionable request that, if granted, will help meet your needs. The request must be phrased as an invitation to collaborate, not as a rigid demand or a consequence.

- **Vague Demand:** "I need you to respect me more." (Too vague; the person does not know what action to take.)
- **Clear Request:** "Would you be willing to put your phone down and confirm you heard the last two sentences when we talk?" (This is a specific, measurable action.)

A request is a request only if the other person is free to say "no" without fear of punishment, guilt, or shame. If you apply coercion or guilt, it is a demand, and a demand is an act of aggression that will destroy trust. You must be prepared to hear "no" and then return to Step 2 to explore the feelings and needs underlying their refusal.

Practical Application: Using NVC in a High-Stakes Scenario

Imagine you are frustrated because your team member, Jordan, consistently arrives five minutes late to key planning meetings, delaying the start time. You feel disrespected and resentful.

The Old Language (Judgmental)	The NVC Framework (Needs-Based)
Judgment / Label: "Jordan, you are so irresponsible and inconsiderate. You need to stop being late all the time. You are wasting everyone's time."	**1. Observation (Neutral Fact):** "Jordan, I have noticed that over the past two weeks, you have arrived five minutes after the scheduled start time for the morning planning meeting."
Masked Feeling / Blame: "I feel completely disrespected by you and your laziness."	**2. Feelings (Pure Emotion):** "When that happens, I feel **frustrated** and a little **anxious**."
Demand / Blaming others: "You need to fix this because it makes me look bad."	**3. Needs (Universal Requirement):** "My need for **efficiency** and **respect for time** is not being met, and I need to feel **confident** in our team's schedule."
Vague Demand: "I expect you to be on time from now on."	**4. Request (Actionable Invitation):** "Would you be willing to commit to arriving by 9:00 AM sharp, or if you can't, let me know by email 30 minutes prior so we can adjust the agenda?"

The difference is structural. The old language targets Jordan's *character*. The NVC language targets your *needs* and a *specific action*. This clarity invites Jordan to partner with you to solve the problem (meeting the need for efficiency), rather than defending their worth against a harsh label.

Training Your Empathy Circuits

The successful application of NVC requires internal work that directly connects with the skills you developed in Book 1 (Focus and Compassion).

To move from Step 2 (Feelings) to Step 3 (Needs), you need **emotional self-reflection**, the ability to accurately identify the specific emotion you are feeling and articulate the underlying need. This emotional self-awareness is essential for healing and growth, and the meta-analytic evidence supports emotional self-reflection for addressing anxiety and depressive symptoms.

Furthermore, NVC strengthens your ability to empathize with the *other* person. After you speak your four steps, you must empathize with their response. Even if they react defensively, you must try to interpret the feeling and need beneath their defensiveness.

- *If Jordan snaps, "I'm not lazy, I was dealing with a crisis!":*
- *Your Empathy Hypothesis:* "It sounds like you are feeling **defensive** and need **understanding** or **acknowledgment** of your difficulty."

This ability to quickly generate a hypothesis about the other person's internal state, what is passing through their mind, relies on **cognitive flexibility** and strengthens the frontal brain activity linked to empathy. This systematic search for the underlying need makes you less likely to attribute malice, reinforcing the work you did to defeat the Hostile Attribution Bias in Book 2.

A New Foundation for Trust

You now have a powerful, actionable model to replace hostile or passive communication. NVC is not a quick fix; it is a fundamental shift in language that takes consistent practice: a lot of unlearning and learning.

By embracing the four steps, Observation, Feelings, Needs, Request, you ensure that all your communications are grounded in facts, driven by genuine human needs, and delivered as an invitation to collaborate. This structured approach builds a durable foundation of mutual trust and respect, ensuring that your words, finally, connect clearly. This is the essential prerequisite for mastering assertiveness and setting boundaries, which is the focus of the next chapter.

CHAPTER 2

ASK FOR WHAT YOU WANT:
USING ASSERTIVENESS AND THE DESC SCRIPT

In the last chapter, you mastered the language of connection using Nonviolent Communication (NVC). You learned to translate hostility and judgment into observations, feelings, and underlying needs. That skill, translating *I feel frustrated* into *My need for efficiency is unmet*, is the essential internal work.

But translation is not enough. You must now learn to deliver that translated message with clarity, conviction, and power. You need the skill of **assertiveness**.

Assertiveness is the crucial bridge between inner calm and external action. It is the ability to stand up for your personal rights, to express your thoughts, feelings, and beliefs in direct, honest, and appropriate ways, while simultaneously respecting the rights and beliefs of others. Without assertiveness, your clear statement of needs (from NVC) can be delivered aggressively (leading to conflict) or passively (leading to your needs being ignored). Both styles are guaranteed to sabotage the health and integrity you are striving to build.

110

This chapter provides the precise, systematic framework for assertive action: the **DESC Script**. This tool allows you to structure high-stakes conversations, eliminating emotional rambling and guaranteeing that your message is delivered clearly, reducing defensiveness, and maximizing your chance of having your interests met.

The Failure of the Extremes: Passive and Aggressive Communication

Most people default to one of two communication extremes, both of which erode self-respect and relational trust:

1. Passive Behavior (The Self-Saboteur)

Passive or nonassertive behavior is characterized by shyness, overly easygoing compliance, and conflict avoidance. The common refrain is, "I will just go with whatever the group decides," even if it costs you time, money, or emotional energy.

- **The Psychological Cost:** This style sends the dangerous message that your thoughts, feelings, and rights are less important than those of other people. In essence, passive behavior teaches others to ignore your wants and needs. This leads to profound feelings of resentment, chronic stress, and a collapse in self-esteem because your actions constantly violate your own integrity and competence. This failure to stand up for one's interests is often a breeding ground for the *anger rumination* you worked to defeat in Book 2, as the repressed frustration festers internally.

2. Aggressive Behavior (The Hostility Trap)

Aggressive behavior involves expressing thoughts and feelings in ways that are insulting, hostile, or demanding. Aggression involves coercion and power over others, using punishment, guilt, or shame to force compliance.

- **The Relational Cost:** While aggression often achieves short-term compliance, the long-term cost is devastating. The message is lost because the listener is too busy reacting to the hostile, aggressive delivery. Aggression instantly triggers defensiveness and alienation, destroying the foundation of mutual trust and respect necessary for a healthy social exchange (as per Social Exchange Theory, Book 3, Chapter 1). This is the very cycle of rudeness and hurtfulness you are working to eliminate.

The Assertive Middle Ground

Assertiveness is the effective and diplomatic communication style because it is founded on **mutual respect**. Being assertive shows that you respect yourself (by standing up for your interests) and that you respect others (by addressing the issue directly and respectfully). Assertiveness reduces stress because you manage conflict constructively instead of letting resentment accumulate. This is the only way to ensure your message is successfully delivered, as people are not distracted by an aggressive delivery style.

The path to learning assertiveness is structural. It requires a precise script to ensure you hit that diplomatic sweet spot every time.

The DESC Script: Your 4-Part Framework

The **DESC Script** is a structured, four-step framework developed to facilitate clear, assertive communication, particularly in challenging situations. It provides a logical flow that prevents emotional tangents and guarantees that you cover the essential elements of an assertive request: the objective facts, your internal experience, the desired change, and the rational benefit of that change.

Using this script is a concrete act of agency. It forces you to pause, regulate your emotions, and engage your rational PFC before responding, a continuation of the control work you mastered in Book 2. By writing out the script and practicing it before a difficult conversation, you ensure that the anxiety of the moment does not hijack your communication.

Step-by-Step Mastery of the DESC Script

D: Describe the Situation or Behavior

The first step requires describing the factual situation or the specific behavior that is causing the problem. This description must be objective, neutral, and devoid of judgment, labels, or emotional interpretation.

- **Connection to NVC (Chapter 2):** This step directly employs the **Observation** principle of NVC. You are providing verifiable data that a neutral camera would record.
- **Why It Works:** Starting with facts, not feelings, decreases defensiveness instantly. The listener cannot argue with a neutral observation.
- **Action Rule:** Use only phrases like, "I noticed that..." or "The facts are..."

Ineffective (Aggressive / Judgmental)	Effective (DESC - Describe)
"You never help me with the setup; I always have to do it myself."	"Jerry, for the last three presentations, I did all of the technical setup by myself, and it took me almost an hour each time."
"You constantly interrupt me."	"I noticed that when I was speaking in the meeting this afternoon, I was interrupted four times."
"This project is a mess."	"The current project timeline shows we are three days behind schedule."

E: Express Your Feelings or Thoughts

The second step is to express your feelings or thoughts about the described situation. This step requires strict adherence to **"I" statements** to avoid triggering defensiveness in the listener.

- **Connection to NVC (Chapter 2):** This employs the **Feelings** principle of NVC, but with a specific focus on phrasing.

- **Why It Works:** Beginning sentences with "You" instantly puts people on the defensive, leading them to stop listening and start formulating a counter-argument. By shifting the focus to your internal state ("I feel..."), you report an internal fact that the listener cannot dispute: they cannot tell you how *you* feel. You invite understanding, not blame.

- **Action Rule:** Use phrases like, "I felt..." or "I think..." or "I am concerned that..."

Ineffective (Blaming / Defensive)	Effective (DESC - Express)
"You make me frustrated and overwhelmed."	"I felt overwhelmed, exhausted, and frustrated having to handle the setup alone."
"You are so disrespectful."	"I feel devalued when I am interrupted, and I find it hard to maintain my focus."
"You clearly don't care."	"I am concerned that this delay will negatively impact our final deliverable date, and I feel anxious about that."

S: Specify the Change You Want (The Request)

The third step is to clearly and specifically articulate the preferred alternative behavior or outcome you want to see happen. Assertiveness requires clarity. The request must be actionable, measurable, and reasonable.

- **Connection to NVC (Chapter 2):** This links directly to the **Request** step of NVC.
  - **Why It Works:** Vague requests ("Be nicer," "Be more helpful") are easily ignored or misinterpreted. A specific request gives the other person a roadmap for success and makes their compliance simple.
  - **Action Rule:** Use phrases like, "I would like us to..." or "I request that..."

Ineffective (Vague / Demanding)	Effective (DESC - Specify)
"You need to contribute more time."	"I would like us to work together on the technical setup for the next presentation, dividing the tasks equally."
"Stop being late."	"I request that we agree to start our morning check-ins exactly at 9:00 AM, regardless of who is present."
"I want you to respect my time."	"I would appreciate it if all work-related texts were sent only between 9 AM and 5 PM on weekdays."

C: Consequences (Specify the Outcome)

The final step is to specify the consequence of the desired action. This consequence should emphasize the **positive benefit** of the change for *both* parties. This frames the request as a collaborative opportunity, not a threat.

- **Why It Works:** This is the motivational hook. It addresses the listener's self-interest. You are showing them, "If we do this, *we* both win." This aligns the request with the principles of Social Exchange Theory, maximizing the perceived reward for compliance.
- **Action Rule:** Focus on shared benefits: "This way we can..." or "The result will be..."

Ineffective (Negative Threat / Guilt)	Effective (DESC - Consequences)
"If you don't help, I will just do it wrong, and it will be your fault."	"This way we can complete the setup in less time, giving us both a chance to gather our thoughts and be more prepared before we present."
"If you don't stop texting me, I will eventually burn out and quit."	"Maintaining these time boundaries will protect my focus and ensure that when I am working, I can give you my best quality performance."
"If we don't start on time, I will feel ignored."	"Starting our check-ins on time will increase our overall meeting efficiency and ensure we leave the room feeling aligned and confident."

The Neurocognitive Power of Assertiveness

The success of the DESC script and assertive communication is not a psychological accident; it is based on predictable neurocognitive responses and measurable behavioral outcomes.

1. Reduced Defensiveness (The "I" Statement Effect)

The use of "I" statements in the Express phase is a highly engineered cognitive intervention. Beginning a sentence with "You" (e.g., "You are rude," "You made me feel") is processed by the brain as an immediate personal threat. This triggers the amygdala and the fight-or-flight response, sending the listener into a defensive mode where cognitive resources are diverted to self-protection.

By contrast, an "I" statement ("I felt frustrated," "I am concerned") is an expression of an internal state. It is a non-threatening report on your reality. It is an invitation to empathy, not a call to arms. Assertiveness, therefore, is crucial for successful communication because the direct, respectful delivery ensures the message is heard, not lost in the static of hostility. This skill directly builds on the control you achieved in Book 2, leveraging your calm to keep the listener calm.

2. Increased Agency and Self-Esteem

Assertiveness is a core communication skill that measurably boosts self-esteem and earns the respect of others.

- **Combating Learned Helplessness:** Recall the feelings of helplessness (Book 1, Chapter 5). Learned helplessness is broken by purposeful action that yields results. When you passively avoid conflict, you reinforce the belief that your needs are not important and that your effort (to communicate) will not produce a desired result. When you successfully execute the DESC script, you prove that your effort *can* successfully advocate for your needs, restoring agency and reducing the chronic stress that results from unmet needs.

- **Measurable Efficacy:** Assertiveness training is a proven method for behavioral change. Studies confirm that participants who undergo assertiveness training significantly improve their assertiveness levels. For example, in one study, 23.5% of participants improved their assertiveness category after the training, compared to only 4% who regressed. This structured practice creates real, measurable improvements in competence.

3. Stress and Anger Reduction

Assertiveness reduces chronic anger and stress. By consistently standing up for your interests in a direct and respectful manner, you prevent the slow, toxic buildup of resentment.

Resentment is often repressed anger, the frustration over unmet needs that you were too passive to voice. This unexpressed frustration can lead to stress and internal emotional buildup, which manifests as irritability, anxiety, and eventual aggressive outbursts (reactive aggression). Assertiveness is the healthy emotional release valve. It prevents the passive erosion of self-worth while avoiding the aggressive explosion. This allows you to control anger and improve your overall coping skills.

Action Plan: Scripting Your Assertive Life

The only way to master the DESC script is through practice. When facing a difficult situation, you must commit to writing out the script first.

Step 1: Identify Your Current Passive/Aggressive Point:

Choose one specific interaction this week where you typically default to passivity (e.g., agreeing to a commitment you do not have time for) or aggression (e.g., snapping at a family member over a recurring chore).

Step 2: Draft the DESC Script:

Write out all four parts clearly and concisely, focusing on short, factual sentences (sentences should average 10–20 words).

- *D*: Describe the fact (e.g., "The laundry basket has been sitting in the hall for three days.")
- *E*: Express your feeling (e.g., "I feel overwhelmed and unsupported when I see it there.")
- *S*: Specify the desired action (e.g., "I request that the laundry be moved to the washing machine before 8 PM each evening.")
- *C*: State the positive consequence (e.g., "This way, the chore can be integrated into our routine, and our common areas will feel calmer.")

Step 3: Practice and Deliver:

Practice the script out loud, maintaining a calm, even tone (leveraging your work from Book 2). The calm tone is essential, as it ensures the message, not the delivery, is the focus.1

By embracing the DESC script, you are choosing intentional action over impulsive reaction. You are moving from a communication style dictated by fear to one defined by self-respect and clarity. This is how you ensure your needs are met while upholding the dignity of others, establishing a durable foundation of relational integrity.

CHAPTER 3

WALK IN THEIR SHOES:
TRAINING YOUR EMPATHY CIRCUITS

You know how to stand your ground now. You can calmly state your needs and ask for what you want using the clear structure of the DESC Script. That is essential self-respect. But when you are dealing with other people, a calm voice and a clear script are only half of the solution.

If you fail to accurately understand the mental state of the person listening to you, your perfectly crafted message can fall apart. Imagine asking a stressed coworker for help: If you do not sense they are overwhelmed, your assertive request, while polite, might feel like the final burden that causes them to snap. You failed to read the room.

We must actively develop **empathy**, the ability to accurately understand what is going on inside another person's head and heart. Empathy is not some innate, fixed quality. It is a trainable cognitive skill. It is the cost of admission for effective communication. If you want your kind speech to land correctly, you must learn to walk in their shoes.

The True Definition: Empathy is a Cognitive Act

We often confuse empathy with other, softer feelings. Let us be precise about the skill we are building:

- **Sympathy** is feeling *pity* or *concern for* someone else's distress. You feel bad for them.
- **Empathy** is the ability to understand and, to a degree, experience their emotional state from *their* viewpoint. It involves both affective (feeling what they feel) and cognitive (knowing what they think) components.
- **Compassion** is the desire to actively *alleviate* the suffering of others. This is an action-oriented response we will focus on in the next chapter.

To communicate clearly, you need the **cognitive side of empathy**, what psychologists call perspective-taking. You need to quickly assess the contextual factors, their underlying feelings, and their likely intentions. This skill is required to make your NVC and DESC scripts successful. You must accurately guess their core needs before you specify your request, or the whole conversation misses the mark.

The Neuroscientific Challenge: Overcoming Rigidity

Why does this feel difficult? Because your brain's default setting promotes *rigidity*, not flexibility.

You are wired to prioritize your own safety and perspective first. When someone is irritable, your brain instantly tries to find a meaning that relates to you: *Did I cause this? Are they mad at me?* This is a remnant of the negativity bias, which can quickly spiral into the **Hostile Attribution Bias**, the automatic assumption that their irritability is aimed at causing you disrespect or harm.

Training empathy is the systematic practice of breaking that rigidity. It is the deliberate engagement of your brain's regulatory structures to run a complex, external social program.

The Brain's Empathy Circuits:

Achieving accurate perspective-taking relies heavily on the frontal lobes of your brain, specifically the areas dedicated to **Theory of Mind**, the ability to attribute mental states, intentions, and beliefs to others.

1. **The Medial Prefrontal Cortex (mPFC) and Dorsolateral Prefrontal Cortex (dlPFC):** These structures are essential for high-level social cognition. Their maturation is associated with an increased capacity to decode complex emotions and interpret the situational factors that drive another person's feelings. When you ask, "Why did she say that?" these areas are working to generate multiple, flexible answers.

2. **The Amygdala and vmPFC:** These areas handle the emotional processing. They allow you to register the *intensity* of the other person's emotion without being completely overwhelmed by it yourself.

When you practice empathy, you are strengthening these neural pathways. You are literally making your brain better at decoding complex human behavior. You are making your social intelligence more flexible and less dependent on your own internal fears. This enhanced cognitive flexibility reduces aggressive reactions because you are less likely to fall into simplistic, blaming assumptions.

Action Tool 1: The Contextual Check

The most damaging assumption you can make during a conflict is that the other person's behavior is 100% about *you*. Most of the time, their visible irritation, defensiveness, or short replies are heavily influenced by factors you cannot see. This tool forces you to pause, regulate (Book 2), and look for those external factors.

Action Focus: The "What's Stressing Them?" Drill

The moment someone responds to you with an unexpected negative emotion: snapping, defensiveness, or a vague withdrawal, you must pause before continuing your assertive communication. Run this quick diagnostic internally:

1. **Isolate the Observation and Feeling (NVC Check):** State the fact and their likely feeling. *Example: "My colleague's voice was sharp when she said 'No' (Observation). She is likely feeling frustrated or stressed (Feeling)."*

2. **Generate a Contextual Hypothesis (The Check):** What is the most plausible, *non-hostile* external factor influencing her irritability? You need at least two options.

   - **Hypothesis A (Simple Stress):** *She is trying to finish a high-priority task, and my question broke her concentration, violating her need for focus.*

o   **Hypothesis B (External Pressure):** *She just had a difficult phone call from a family member or a tense exchange with her manager.*

3. **Formulate the Empathic Need:** Based on your hypothesis, what is her probable unmet universal need? *Example: If Hypothesis A is true, her need is for* **autonomy** *and* **focus.**

This exercise strengthens the part of your brain that interprets situational factors. By simulating the external pressures on them, you make it less likely you will attribute their behavior to intentional malice aimed at you. This preserves your internal calm, reinforces the work you did to defeat the Hostile Attribution Bias (Book 2), and allows you to respond with appropriate kindness rather than defensiveness.

Action Tool 2: The Perspective Rehearsal

To cement true empathy, you must actively practice taking the other person's perspective (Perspective Rehearsal). This is often used in social skills training because it forces your brain to generate a full internal narrative that is not your own. You are running a script from their point of view.

Action Focus: Scripting Their Reality

Choose a recent interaction where you felt frustrated or misunderstood, and then script the scenario from the other person's exact viewpoint. You are applying the NVC steps (Observation, Feeling, Need) to *them*, based on what *they* saw you do.

1. **Their Observation:** What specific, factual actions did they see you take? *Example: "I saw him come home late and immediately start watching television on the sofa."*

2. **Their Feeling:** What emotion did that observation likely trigger in them? *Example: "I felt overwhelmed and anxious."*

3. **Their Need:** What universal human need was unmet by your action? *Example: "My need for* **partnership** *and* **predictability** *was not met, because I was left with the entire load of evening chores."*

This intentional effort transforms the conflict in your mind. You move from the belief "They are mad at me because I am bad" to the realization "They are anxious because their need for predictability is not met." This shift changes the entire nature of the problem, moving it from a personal attack to a clash of systems, which is something you can solve constructively.

The power of your assertive communication (DESC Script) relies entirely on the accuracy of your empathy training. You cannot successfully complete Step S (Specify) and Step C (Consequences) without first engaging your empathy circuits.

DESC Step	Empathy is Required Because...
D: Describe	You must describe the situation using language that does not trigger their defensiveness. Empathy helps you choose neutral words.
S: Specify the Request	You must ensure your request is *actionable* for them and does not violate a core need of theirs (e.g., their need for autonomy, control, or time). If you empathize that they are overwhelmed (Need: **Ease**), you must revise your request to minimize the burden.
C: Specify the Consequences	The consequence must focus on a **shared benefit** that appeals to *their* interests and needs (Social Exchange Theory, Book 3, Chapter 1). Empathy tells you what they value most: time, peace, or efficiency. You frame the consequence to address that value.

This continuous cross-checking ensures that your assertive message is not just delivered clearly, but strategically. When you demonstrate that you understand and respect the other person's needs, even while standing up for your own, you increase the likelihood of collaboration and compliance. This ability to express yourself effectively while respecting the other person's rights and beliefs is what boosts your self-esteem and, crucially, earns their respect, making them more willing to meet your request.

The Flexible Mind

Empathy is the key skill that transforms blunt honesty into kind, effective communication. It moves your mind away from the rigidity of self-centered fear and into the flexibility required for sophisticated social behavior.

By engaging in Contextual Checks and Perspective Rehearsals, you are strengthening the neural pathways of social cognition. You are learning to read the human world with accuracy, ensuring that your kind speech is not only well-intentioned but profoundly effective. This ability to walk in their shoes is the final prerequisite before we address the deepest internal work: moving past judgment and into compassion and acceptance, the topic of the next essential chapter.

CHAPTER 4
MOVE PAST JUDGMENT:
SHIFTING TO COMPASSION AND ACCEPTANCE

You have built the essential structure for external kindness. You can empathize with the context and needs of others (Chapter 4), and you can communicate your own needs with clarity and respect (Chapter 3). You are now adept at handling the exchange of information.

But communication is only sustainable if it is fueled by a generous internal state. If you approach every conversation with a demanding, critical, or judgmental internal attitude, your external kindness will feel forced and eventually deplete you. The inner critic, that voice you started challenging in Book 1, often survives by pointing its finger at others, constantly evaluating them against an impossible standard of "shoulds" and "oughts."

To move past this demanding state, you must cultivate **compassion** and **acceptance**. This involves applying the same self-kindness you practiced in Book 1, but extending it outward. Compassion is not merely a soft feeling; it is a powerful emotional response that is measurable in the brain's reward circuits. It is the action-oriented desire to alleviate suffering, both your own and that of others. By intentionally replacing judgment with acceptance, you build an internal reservoir of emotional resilience that makes kind speech genuine and effortless.

The Internal Cost of Judgment

Judgment is a rigid thinking habit. It involves imposing moralistic, absolute standards on others, often rooted in your own fears, insecurities, or cultural conditioning. When you judge, you eliminate nuance. You assign fixed, negative labels to complex human behavior (e.g., "They are lazy," "They are incompetent," or "They are malicious").

This habit carries three major costs:

1. **Fueling Cognitive Rigidity:** Judgment is a form of the cognitive distortion **Labeling** (Book 1). By constantly labeling others, you reinforce the rigid, black-and-white thinking that your PFC is trying to overcome. This prevents the flexible, nuanced thinking required for empathy and problem-solving.

2. **Activating Stress:** A demanding, judgmental mind is a mind under constant stress. When others fail to meet your impossible standards, you feel anger and resentment, triggering the physiological surge you worked to control in Book 2.

3. **Blocking Connection:** Judgment eliminates the possibility of connection. When you look at someone through a judgmental lens, you are incapable of seeing their underlying human need (NVC, Chapter 2). This prevents the possibility of collaboration and ensures that conflict is met with defensiveness, not trust.

The shift from judgment to compassion is the ultimate antidote to these costs. You are changing the fundamental lens through which you view yourself and others.

The Scientific Power of Compassion

While empathy is understanding another's feelings, **compassion** is the emotional response that includes a motivation or desire to alleviate that suffering. Compassion is not abstract; it is a robust, rewarding neurological experience.

Research into the neural correlates of compassion reveals a fascinating truth: compassion is reinforced by your brain's own reward system.

- **Reward Circuit Activation:** Studies indicate that compassion is associated with activity in specific brain regions linked to reward, most notably the **right caudate nucleus**. This area is part of the striatum, which is central to motivation and positive reinforcement (the same area where dopamine dampening leads to learned helplessness, Book 1, Chapter 5).

- **Motivation for Prosociality:** People who display lower compassion tend to show reduced neural activity or gray matter volume in these reward areas. This suggests that compassion is an intrinsically motivating state. When you successfully engage in compassionate action or thought, your brain registers a neurochemical reward, reinforcing the behavior.

By actively cultivating compassion, you are building a behavior that is chemically self-sustaining. Compassion is not a sacrifice; it is a highly rewarded state that strengthens your ability to engage in prosocial, kind behavior.

Action Tool 1: Cultivating Self-Compassion with LKM

You must first direct compassion inward. You cannot offer acceptance to others that you deny to yourself. The inner critic's most damaging work is punishing you for perceived failures. You must replace this criticism with kindness.

The most effective, evidence-based technique for cultivating self-compassion is **Loving-Kindness Meditation (LKM)**, which you were introduced to in Book 1, Chapter 6. LKM uses the repetition of specific phrases to generate feelings of warmth and acceptance, providing a structured way to interrupt cycles of self-judgment and criticism.

Action Focus: Extending the Self-Compassion Script

Practice LKM for ten uninterrupted minutes daily.

1. **Find Calm:** Start by engaging deep, slow, diaphragmatic breathing (4-7-8 method, Book 2) to downregulate your stress level and create mental space.

2. **Target the Self:** Begin by silently repeating the self-compassion script, feeling the warmth in your chest.

    - *Script:* "May I accept myself as I am right now. May I be safe and protected. May I be peaceful and at ease. May I be kind to myself."

3. **Extend to Others (The Compassion Bridge):** Once the feeling of warmth is stable and focused on yourself, expand the circle outward, applying the exact same warmth and acceptance to others.

    ○ *First, a neutral person:* "May this person also be safe and peaceful."

    ○ *Second, a person in conflict:* Focus on someone you often judge or who frustrates you. Repeat the phrases, focusing on their humanity: "May this person also find acceptance. May they be free from suffering."

The Internal Shift: This practice forces you to confront the rigidity of your judgment. When you direct kindness toward a difficult person, you bypass the labels you assigned them and access the core human being underneath. This trains your brain to choose acceptance over criticism, building profound emotional resilience.

Action Tool 2: The Acceptance Audit

Compassion is applied through the lens of acceptance. Acceptance is the acknowledgment of reality as it is, without the demand that it be different. Judgment is the demand that reality conform to your expectations ("It shouldn't be this way").

The **Acceptance Audit** is a powerful cognitive tool that uses the NVC framework (Chapter 2) to challenge the "shoulds" and shift to reality.

The Three Steps of the Acceptance Audit:

1. **Identify the Judgment (The Should Statement):** Pinpoint the absolute demand you are placing on yourself or others. *Example: "My colleague **should** know how to do this simple task without asking me."* (The judgment is that they are incompetent, and they are violating your standard of expertise.)

2. **Identify the Unmet Need:** Beneath the judgment, what is the *real* need being violated? *Example: Your need is for **ease**, **autonomy** (not to be interrupted), and **competence** (you need confidence in the team's ability).*

3. **Reframe to Acceptance and Action:** State the reality without judgment, and then focus on addressing the need constructively.

Judgmental Thought	Factual Acceptance	Compassionate Action (NVC / DESC)
"He **shouldn't** interrupt me; he's so rude."	*Acceptance:* "The reality is that he interrupted me. He likely needs **clarity** (Empathy Check, Chapter 4) and has poor boundary skills."	*Action:* I will use the DESC script to set an assertive time boundary, meeting my need for **focus** without labeling him as rude.
"I **should** be perfect on this assignment; I'm failing."	*Acceptance:* "The reality is that I am imperfect. I made a mistake, but this is a learning opportunity."	*Action:* I will apply self-compassion (LKM) and initiate a SMART goal (Book 1, Chapter 5) to correct the mistake.

By reframing the judgment as an unmet need that requires a constructive solution, you move your focus from angry, static criticism to dynamic problem-solving. This process actively supports the flexibility of your PFC, allowing you to deal with conflict lucidly and effectively.

The Integration of Acceptance and Clarity

The work in this chapter ensures that the assertive communication models from Chapter 3 are delivered with genuine connection, not cold efficiency.

- **Assertiveness with Care:** When you operate from acceptance, your DESC script naturally becomes more empathetic. You can describe a colleague's late submission factually, express your frustration, and specify a deadline change, all while acknowledging the reality that they may be struggling with external stress (Contextual Empathy Check, Chapter 4). This combination of **firm clarity and compassionate acceptance** is the highest form of professional communication.

- **The Power of Calm:** Acceptance is deeply supported by the physiological regulation you mastered in Book 2. Diaphragmatic breathing helps downregulate overall stress levels, slowing your thoughts and creating the mental space needed to intentionally replace critical inner dialogue with rational, compassionate self-talk.

The intentional practice of acceptance is how you move beyond the rigid self-centeredness of negative habits. You are building an inner strength that allows you to tolerate the inevitable imperfections of yourself and others without collapsing into judgment or reactive anger. This durable shift makes kind speech not just an external act, but a natural outflow of your compassionate internal state. You are ready to apply this acceptance to the ultimate challenge: repairing broken trust.

CHAPTER 5

MEND THE RIFT:

USING KIND DIALOGUE TO REPAIR CONFLICT

You have put in the work. You have achieved profound internal quiet. You can now calm your body when provoked, you refuse to assume the worst intent in others, and you can state your needs clearly using the DESC Script.

But let us be honest: you are human. You will slip up. You will raise your voice when you are tired. You will say something thoughtless when you are stressed. Hurtful words will escape, trust will be violated, and the emotional security of your relationship will rupture.

The measure of your newfound mastery is not how well you avoid these mistakes. It is how effectively you **repair** them. A rupture is an inevitability. A failure to repair is a choice. If you leave the damage untouched, the conflict festers, driving the relationship back toward the hostility and defensiveness you worked so hard to eliminate.

This chapter provides the structured, kind dialogue necessary for relational repair. It requires genuine accountability, focused listening, and a commitment to rebuilding emotional security. When handled correctly, the repair process transforms conflict from a destructive event into a powerful opportunity to strengthen trust.

130

When you speak hurtful words, the damage is not just emotional. It is neurological. Hurt triggers the same fear response as a physical threat. The brain registers a rupture in the relationship as a violation of safety, activating the amygdala and sending the body into stress mode.

An apology that includes an excuse or a condition ("I'm sorry you felt that way, *but* I was stressed") completely fails to mend the rift. Why? Because it denies the listener's reality. It sends the message that their feelings are less valid than your justification. This destroys the accountability required to restore trust.

The science of effective repair confirms a critical truth: you must take responsibility for the **impact** of your words, independent of your initial intent. You might have *intended* to sound only direct, but if your words were *perceived* as rude and hostile, you are fully accountable for the resulting pain. This act of owning the consequence is what weaves connection back into the interaction and begins the work of rebuilding security.

Action Tool 1: The Accountable Apology

The typical apology focuses on the speaker's feelings ("I feel bad"). The accountable apology focuses exclusively on the listener's violated needs. It uses the language of NVC (Chapter 2) and the structure of assertiveness (Chapter 3) to achieve maximum clarity and accountability.

An effective apology must be structured in three sequential, non-negotiable parts. You must never use the word "but" or any phrase that shifts blame to the listener ("if you hadn't...").

1. Acknowledge the Specific Behavior (D: Describe)

Start by factually describing the specific behavior you regret. This shows the listener that you were paying attention, that you understand exactly what you did wrong, and that you are taking ownership of the action, not just the feeling.

- **Ineffective (Vague):** "I'm sorry I was mean earlier."
- **Accountable (Specific):** "I acknowledge that I raised my voice above a respectful volume, and I used the generalizing phrase, 'You always leave me to do this work.' That specific action was mine." (This is a factual statement of the precise, regretted behavior.)

2. Express Regret for the Resulting Feeling and Need (E: Express & Empathy)

Express genuine regret for the *impact* your action had on the other person, explicitly linking their feeling to their underlying human need. This step engages your empathy circuits (Chapter 4) and validates their vulnerability.

- **Ineffective (Conditional):** "I'm sorry you were sensitive about what I said."
- **Accountable (Empathic):** "I truly regret that my loud voice and generalizing language caused you to feel humiliated and deeply invalidated. I understand that your core need for **respect** and **acknowledgment of your effort** was severely violated by my words."

When you identify and validate the core universal human need (e.g., respect, safety, value), the listener often experiences an immediate emotional release. They feel heard, which is the necessary prerequisite for them to lower their defensive wall.

3. State a Future Commitment (S & C: Specify and Consequences)

End by stating a clear, specific, and measurable commitment to a different behavior next time. This is the crucial step that replaces the past failure with a clear path for future success and earns back trust. Trust is built not on words, but on predictable, positive behavior.

- **Ineffective (Vague Promise):** "I promise I'll try to be better in the future."
- **Accountable (Action-Oriented):** "My commitment is this: Next time I feel frustrated by the workload, I will first initiate the 4-7-8 breathing protocol, and I will then use the DESC script to state my needs factually. I commit to never using generalizing or judgmental language again. This is how I will rebuild our trust, ensuring our communication is constructive."

This structured, accountable apology closes the gap created by the hostility. It transforms the moment of rupture into a process of self-correction, which the listener can observe and trust.

Action Tool 2: De-escalating Post-Conflict Defensiveness

Even after a perfect apology, the other person may remain defensive, emotional, or resistant to letting go of the conflict. This is usually because their core need still feels vulnerable or exposed. If you continue to defend yourself here, you restart the conflict.

To move past this residual defensiveness, you must use empathy and reflective listening as a de-escalation tool. This requires you to silence your own narrative and focus entirely on confirming the other person's internal reality.

Action Focus: Reflecting the Unmet Need

When the other person continues to voice frustration or blame, do not defend your past action. Instead, reflect back their probable feeling and need until they feel entirely heard.

1. **Listen Past the Blame:** Listen past the words of judgment ("You are so selfish!") to the underlying, universal human need (e.g., "They need **fairness** or **support**").

2. **Reflect and Validate:** Use a soft, non-judgmental tone to reflect their internal state back to them. Frame it as a question to confirm your empathy check. *Example: "It sounds like you are still feeling extremely **angry** and **unsupported**, and your core need for **equity** in our workload is completely unmet. Is that what you are telling me?"*

The Scientific Result: When a person hears their deepest need validated without argument, the emotional intensity often dissipates instantly. NVC studies highlight that listening for and validating the need is the most powerful method for getting past defensiveness and opening the door to collaboration. By reflecting their reality, you fulfill the fundamental human need to be understood. Only once this need is met can they shift from emotional reaction to rational problem-solving.

The Integration of Repair: From Hostility to Competence

Repair is the ultimate integration test for all the skills you have learned in the first two books. A successful repair process is sequential and systematic:

1. Preventing the Second Surge (Book 2 Mastery)

- **Failure Point:** You feel the heat of their continued anger.
- **Intervention:** Immediately engage the **4-7-8 breathing protocol** to prevent your own emotional re-surge. Use physiological regulation to keep your PFC online so you can listen calmly, without engaging their hostility defensively.

2. Auditing the Damage (Book 1 & 2 Mastery)

- **Failure Point:** You contributed to the rupture with hostile language.

- **Intervention:** Interrupt any **rumination** (Book 2, Chapter 3). Then, apply the **TCT** and **Reality Testing** (Book 1, Chapter 3 and Book 2, Chapter 4) to your own thoughts: *Did I use **Labeling**? Was my generalization (**always/never**) a cognitive distortion?* This audit prepares you for the honest, factual apology (Action Tool 1).

3. Initiating Collaboration (Book 3 Mastery)

- **Failure Point:** You need to transition from apology to a solution.

- **Intervention:** Once the Accountable Apology is delivered and their need is reflected and validated (Action Tool 2), immediately initiate the **5-Step Structured Problem-Solving Model** (Book 2, Chapter 5). The problem is no longer the argument; the problem is the *unmet need* (e.g., the need for equity in chores). The focus shifts from blame to a measurable, constructive action plan.

The ultimate outcome of this sequence is moving both parties away from the volatile, affective outburst (reactive aggression) toward the controlled, planned response. Problem-solving interventions have been shown to increase self-control, providing individuals with alternative, constructive strategies for responding to conflict, which measurably reduces aggressive behavior.

Trust Built Through Accountability

The ability to successfully repair conflict transforms relationships. Every time you successfully navigate a breakdown using structured accountability and empathetic listening, you reinforce the relationship's foundation of mutual trust.

The skills you learned in this book, NVC, the DESC script, and Empathy Training, are designed precisely for this moment: to ensure that when your integrity is tested, you possess the language and the internal control to uphold it. You are proving that your commitment to self-respect and relational health is stronger than your impulse to be right. This mastery of repair is the definitive sign that you have achieved connection through clarity, setting the stage for the next deep internal work: building inner strength through gratitude.

CONCLUSION
COMMUNICATE WITH CONNECTION: YOUR FOUNDATION FOR MUTUAL TRUST

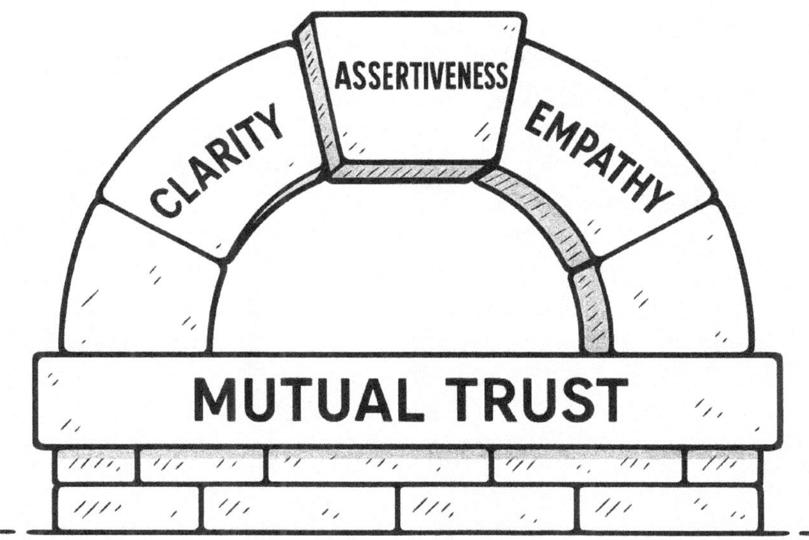

You have completed the essential work of mastering communication. This book, *Connect Clearly*, moved you from reacting with hurtful words and defensive silence to engaging with assertive clarity and compassionate understanding. You have fundamentally restructured the way you speak, listen, and interact.

This transformation, from hostility to clear connection, is the bedrock for all healthy relationships. It is the guarantee that your words will build trust, not erode it. The ultimate measure of this mastery is the durability of the foundation you have established: a foundation built on mutual respect, vulnerability, and the predictable use of structured language.

Let us review the integrated skills you have gained, confirming how the combination of NVC, assertiveness, and empathy ensures that kind speech becomes your resilient and reliable default.

The success of your new communication style is due to its systematic, three-part structure. You learned to use each skill in sequence, leveraging your internal calm (Book 2) to achieve external clarity.

1. The Clarity of Needs-Based Dialogue (NVC)

You began by rejecting the language of judgment and blame that characterized your past hurtful habits.

- **The Action:** You mastered the **Four Steps of Nonviolent Communication (NVC)**, translating vague frustration into **Observation, Feeling, Need, and Request**. You learned that anger or frustration is simply a signal that a universal human need (e.g., for safety, connection, or autonomy) is unmet.

- **The Relational Effect:** By speaking in terms of verifiable facts and genuine human needs, you bypass the listener's defensiveness. This invites collaboration instead of resistance, making the listener more receptive to your message and fostering a stronger foundation of mutual trust. Research shows that NVC training increases empathy and reduces interpersonal tension, proving the effectiveness of this needs-based structure.

2. The Power of Respectful Action (Assertiveness)

Knowing your needs is not enough; you must deliver them with conviction. Assertiveness is the core skill that ensures your needs are met while upholding the dignity of others.

- **The Action:** You mastered the **DESC Script** (Describe, Express, Specify, Consequences) for managing high-stakes conversations. This structured, sequential framework forces you to deliver your requests directly, honestly, and respectfully, avoiding the pitfalls of passive avoidance or aggressive demands.

- **The Psychological Effect:** Assertiveness is a critical coping skill that reduces stress and prevents the toxic buildup of resentment (unexpressed anger) that fuels future hostile outbursts. By standing up for your rights and interests, you confirm to yourself and others that your needs are important. This action reinforces agency, which you learned is vital for countering learned helplessness (Book 1, Chapter 5), and it measurably boosts self-esteem.

3. The Nuance of Perspective-Taking (Empathy and Acceptance)

The structure of your communication is only successful if it is fueled by internal acceptance and genuine understanding of the other person.

- **The Action:** You trained your **Empathy Circuits** by practicing **Contextual Checks** and **Perspective Rehearsal** (Chapter 4). This actively strengthens the frontal lobe areas responsible for "theory of mind", the ability to understand the situational and social factors driving the other person's behavior.

- **The Emotional Effect:** This training makes you less susceptible to the Hostile Attribution Bias (Book 2), ensuring you respond to a person's irritability with nuance and understanding, rather than immediate, defensive hostility. Furthermore, by practicing **Compassion and Acceptance** (Chapter 5), you moved past internal judgment and built a self-sustaining emotional reserve, fueled by the neurochemical rewards of kindness. This internal state makes your external kind speech feel authentic, not forced.

Relational Integrity: The Ultimate Outcome

The consistent application of these structured verbal tools builds a durable foundation of **mutual trust**. This integrity is what defines the long-term success of your new habits.

- **Predictability:** Assertive communication is predictable. People trust you because they know what you mean, they know you will not resort to passive-aggression, and they know you will not explode into reactive rage. This clarity is a high reward in the social exchange (Social Exchange Theory, Book 5), and it stabilizes your relationships.

- **Safety in Conflict:** Crucially, you mastered the dialogue necessary for **Relational Repair** (Chapter 6). By committing to the Accountable Apology, focusing on the specific behavior and the violated need, you proved that your commitment to integrity is stronger than your impulse to be right. This skill transforms conflict from a destructive threat into a strengthening opportunity.

The mastery of kind speech ensures that the hard-won internal calm you secured in Book 1 and Book 2 is protected. Your words will no longer sabotage your peace.

The next challenge, addressed in Book 4, is to deepen the internal well of emotional strength, ensuring that your resilience is not reliant on the behavior of others. We turn now to **gratitude**, a powerful, scientific intervention that further reduces stress hormones, increases physical health, and cements the positive focus you started building. This internal strengthening ensures your kind speech flows from a deep, unwavering source of inner abundance.

REFLECTION QUESTIONS

1. Describe a recent high-stakes conversation. Did you use pure feeling words (e.g., frustrated) or masked judgment words (e.g., ignored)? Use the NVC format to clearly restate your true underlying unmet need.

2. Write down an example where you successfully used the **DESC script** to deliver an assertive boundary. Specifically, how did the **Consequences** phase appeal to the other person's interests (using empathy)?

3. Describe a time this week when someone responded to you with unexpected anger or irritation. What **Contextual Hypothesis** did you generate (Chapter 4) to neutralize the hostile attribution bias, and what unmet need did you guess was driving their behavior?

4. Describe a moment where you felt an impulse to judge a colleague or friend. How did you apply the **Acceptance Audit** (Chapter 5) to move your mind from judgment to focusing on objective reality and constructive action?

5. Reflecting on a recent conflict, how did you use the three steps of the **Accountable Apology** (Chapter 6) to mend the rift? What specific commitment did you make for future behavior to rebuild trust?

BOOK FOUR

BUILD INNER STRENGTH:
DAILY HABITS FOR PRACTICING GRATITUDE

INTRODUCTION

GRATITUDE IS MORE THAN THANKS: DEFINING THE CLINICAL TOOL

You have secured the external world. You have learned to regulate your impulses (Book 2) and to communicate with assertive clarity (Book 3). You can handle conflict. But to ensure these skills are resilient and durable, to make sure you do not regress when the next big stressor hits, you must deepen your inner strength.

This final stage of internal repair is not about fixing a flaw; it is about building a psychological asset: **gratitude**.

For many, gratitude is simply a polite social custom, saying thank you for a gift or a service. In this book, we define gratitude not as a fleeting good feeling, but as a specific, evidence-based **psychological intervention**. This is a commitment to a structured mental habit that actively rewires your brain, reduces your stress hormones, and dramatically increases your emotional resilience.

If you struggle with lingering anxiety, persistent worry, or a feeling that life is constantly unfair, gratitude is your most powerful tool for counteracting those states. The goal is to fundamentally shift the balance of your internal world so that you are reliably nourished by what you have, rather than depleted by what you lack.

The Scientific Deficit: The Bias Against Abundance

To understand the power of gratitude, we must revisit the fundamental bias you first encountered in Book 1: the **negativity bias**.

Your brain is designed to attend to, learn from, and dwell on negative information far more than positive information. This bias serves as an ancient survival mechanism, but in modern life, it ensures that your mind operates like a **Mental Filter** (a cognitive distortion from Book 1): it automatically seeks out perceived threats, inadequacies, and losses while ignoring or minimizing experiences of contentment and abundance.

This focus on lack and threat has three major costs that gratitude directly addresses:

1. **Emotional Depletion:** The constant focus on what is wrong or missing sustains a low-level state of dissatisfaction, which is emotionally draining and contributes to depressive and anxious behaviors.

2. **Toxic Comparison:** When focused on lack, the mind defaults to toxic emotions like envy, jealousy, and resentment. You compare your current state (what you lack) to others, which instantly triggers feelings of inadequacy and self-judgment.

3. **Sustained Stress Chemistry:** The internal feeling of constant threat keeps your stress system on high alert. This prevents the physiological calm (high HRV, low heart rate) you worked so hard to achieve in Book 2 from becoming your default state.

Gratitude is the direct, intentional counter-measure to this chemical and cognitive default. It is a behavioral strategy that forces the mind to prioritize and process positive data, strengthening the "Velcro" for the good that you started building with the HEAL method.

Gratitude as a Clinical Intervention

The benefits of engaging in gratitude practices are not speculative; they are measurable in large-scale clinical meta-analyses. Scientific studies confirm that structured gratitude interventions serve as a powerful therapeutic complement for addressing chronic negative emotional states.

1. Measurable Reductions in Anxiety and Depression

Meta-analytic evidence has quantified the impact of consistent gratitude practice on mental health indicators:

- **Anxiety Symptoms:** Participants who incorporated gratitude interventions experienced a measurable decrease in anxiety symptoms, with a **7.76% lower Generalized Anxiety Disorder (GAD-7) score** than control groups.

- **Depression Symptoms:** The same analysis showed that gratitude interventions led to a significant reduction in depressive symptoms, with a **6.89% lower Patient Health Questionnaire-9 (PHQ-9) score** than control groups.

These statistics confirm that deliberate acts of gratitude are not superficial mood boosters. They are functional psychological actions that reduce the burden of anxiety and depression, increase overall positive mood, and lead to greater feelings of life satisfaction.

2. Enhancing Emotional Resilience

Gratitude practices are strongly correlated with **resilience**, the ability to bounce back quickly from adversity. By consistently focusing on what is present and good, gratitude builds a firewall against toxic emotions. It forces the brain to look for resources rather than focusing only on loss, which is essential for coping with difficult circumstances with a broader perspective and greater awareness.

This consistent effort to appreciate what remains, rather than dwelling on what is missing, leads to a sustained increase in overall optimism and emotional strength. This means that when a conflict inevitably arises (Book 3), you approach it from a place of sufficiency, not emotional neediness.

The Mechanism of Action: Rewiring Your Focus

The core mechanism by which gratitude works is through the alteration of **selective attention.**

If you commit to recording something positive that occurred today (such as through journaling), your brain naturally begins to actively **scan and notice** those good things in your life throughout the day. This anticipatory effect, knowing you will reflect on the good later, actively overrides the mental filter of the negativity bias.

This structured scanning forces your brain to register positive experiences: the moment of kindness received, the success achieved, the physical comfort felt. This intentional, repeated focus on positive data facilitates the necessary neuroplastic change (HEAL method, Book 1), strengthening the neural pathways that promote joy and contentment. The brain literally becomes more sensitized to positive input.

The Two Pillars of Gratitude Practice

To achieve these measurable benefits, gratitude must be practiced in structured ways. This book focuses on the two most effective, evidence-based interventions:

1. **Written Consistency (Gratitude Journaling):** This practice, explored in Chapter 2, provides the daily, low-friction tool necessary to maintain consistency and train your selective attention. Structured journaling is essential for altering daily cognitive habits and tracking physical benefits like improved sleep.

2. **Relational Depth (Appreciation Letters):** This intensive practice, covered in Chapter 4, targets specific social bonds. Research indicates that gratitude letters produce more intense immediate benefits and longer-lasting effects than journaling because they activate stronger social cognition processes, leading to more robust neuroplastic changes in the brain's social pathways.

This dual approach ensures you build both a deep, stable internal resource and strong, positive external relationships.

Integrating Gratitude into Your New Self

The practices in this book are not isolated. They reinforce every skill you have learned so far, ensuring the entire system remains resilient:

- **Supports Calm (Book 2):** Gratitude provides a powerful, natural detox for the stress system. By reducing the primary stress hormone, **cortisol** (Chapter 3), gratitude lowers the baseline physiological arousal in your body. This supports the vagal tone and higher HRV you established in Book 2, making it easier to stay regulated and calm when conflict hits.

- **Fuels Assertiveness (Book 3):** When you approach a difficult conversation from a place of gratitude, acknowledging the resources you have, you are less likely to demand, blame, or regress into hostility. Gratitude is the generous emotional state that makes clear, kind, and assertive communication genuine.

- **Increases Prosocial Action:** Gratitude is a direct predictor of prosocial behavior, the desire to help and share with others (Chapter 6). When you feel grateful for the support you receive, you are chemically and cognitively motivated to repay that kindness, creating a positive, reciprocal loop in your social exchanges.

The commitment to gratitude is the final, essential step in building an inner strength that is independent of circumstance. You are seizing control of your emotional destiny by choosing to focus on abundance. This simple daily habit is the key to maintaining your new outlook and health.

CHAPTER 1

WRITE IT DOWN: STARTING YOUR EVIDENCE-BASED GRATITUDE JOURNAL

In Book 1, you learned how the brain defaults to focusing on negativity, the **negativity bias**, because it is wired for survival. This natural filter causes you to prioritize worries, perceived threats, and losses over moments of contentment. If you do not actively intervene, those brief positive moments slide right off, like water on Teflon.

The commitment to structured **gratitude journaling** is the simplest, most accessible, and most consistent way to permanently fix this problem. It is not just about writing a list of things you are thankful for; it is an evidence-based intervention that forces your brain to redirect its attention. The simple daily act of writing down what is good trains your mind to scan your environment for positive data, fundamentally rewiring your focus.

This chapter is your practical guide to starting and sustaining an evidence-based gratitude journal. We will define the structure, explain why consistency matters, and detail how moving beyond simple lists of objects to genuine relational depth is what creates lasting neuroplastic change.

The Scientific Power of Selective Attention

The success of gratitude journaling lies in its capacity to alter your **selective attention**.

Selective attention is the cognitive process that allows you to focus on specific stimuli while filtering out others. If you are anxious, your selective attention filters for potential threats. If you are in a state of gratitude, your selective attention shifts to filter for experiences of abundance and well-being.

- **The Anticipatory Effect:** When you commit to a gratitude journal, your brain knows, consciously or unconsciously, that it will have to record something positive later in the day. This knowledge forces your brain to begin noticing those good things throughout the day, even before you sit down to write. This systematic "scanning" for positive data actively overrides the **Mental Filter**, the cognitive distortion that previously caused you to ignore all positive elements in a situation (Book 1, Chapter 2).

- **Rewiring the Focus:** By repeatedly engaging this positive selective attention, you create a process of positive sensitization. This process strengthens the neural pathways that promote joy and contentment (HEAL method, Book 1), making your brain faster and more efficient at registering and holding onto beneficial experiences.

The journal is simply the tool that forces this intentional, powerful cognitive shift. Without the written commitment, the positive moments remain fleeting and fail to integrate into your long-term emotional resilience.

Structuring Your Evidence-Based Journal

For the gratitude journal to work as a clinical intervention, it must be structured. Inconsistent or vague entries ("I'm grateful for my family") fail to provide the mind with the rich, detailed focus needed to facilitate real neuroplastic change. The intensity of focus is what moves the experience from a momentary good feeling to a durable psychological trait.

Rule 1: Consistency is the Neuroplastic Key

For maximum impact, the journal should be a consistent practice. Research has found that consistency in practice significantly increases positive affect and overall life satisfaction.

- **Frequency:** While some studies use weekly journaling, a daily commitment provides the greatest advantage for training selective attention and sustaining the necessary focus. The goal is to build a reliable habit.
- **Timing:** Dedicate a specific time each day, such as before bed or immediately upon waking, to writing your entries. This commitment transforms the practice into an automatic routine, reducing the resistance that comes with needing to "find time."

Rule 2: Go for Depth, Not Just Quantity

You must move beyond simple lists of objects (e.g., "Food, Car, House"). Effective journaling requires you to focus on the *why* and the *how* of the event, engaging deeper emotional and cognitive processes.

For each entry, you must answer these three questions:

1. **What:** State the specific event, interaction, or comfort you are grateful for. (Example: "The conversation I had with my colleague, Sarah, this afternoon.")
2. **Why:** Explain the *cause* of the good feeling and how the event was beneficial to you. (Example: "Because she actively listened to my new idea and gave me constructive feedback that improved the pitch.")
3. **How:** Describe the feeling and sensation in detail. This connects the cognitive thought to the physical body, which is essential for emotional absorption (HEAL method, Book 1). (Example: "I felt a deep sense of validation and competence. I felt the physical tension leave my shoulders when she offered her support.")

This sustained focus on the depth of the experience, rather than superficial listing, facilitates the neural change required to hardwire beneficial experiences into your emotional bank.

Rule 3: Target Effort and Intent (Relational Focus)

To maximize the benefits of gratitude, you must often focus on the effort or intent of other people, rather than just material objects. This is a critical step that strengthens social cognition and relational bonds.

- **Focus on Agency:** Instead of simply writing "I am grateful for my comfortable bed," write: "I am grateful that my partner made the effort to tidy the room before I came to bed, demonstrating their care and commitment to my comfort."
- **Focus on Effort:** Instead of, "The coffee was good," write: "I am grateful for the dedication of the barista who crafted that drink perfectly, providing me with a moment of peaceful enjoyment this morning."

By targeting the agency and effort of others, you are reinforcing the values of kindness and prosocial behavior in your social world. You are acknowledging that positive outcomes are often the result of intentional effort, not just luck.

Measurable Health Benefits: Sleep and Stress

The sustained practice of gratitude journaling yields quantifiable benefits that extend far beyond mood, directly impacting your physical wellness. This provides objective proof that your cognitive practice is changing your body.

1. Improved Sleep Quality

Chronic negativity, rumination, and anxiety are notorious for disrupting sleep, often by sustaining high heart rates and active minds (Book 2). Gratitude directly counteracts this.

- **The Mechanism:** By intentionally shifting your focus to positive experiences before bed, you naturally lower the psychological arousal that keeps you awake. This helps to soothe a racing heart and calm frazzled nerves.
- **The Proof:** Studies indicate that people who consistently practice gratitude journaling report **better quality sleep** and often fall asleep in a shorter period of time. This improvement in sleep is a direct, measurable benefit that reinforces the efficacy of the intervention. Better sleep, in turn, strengthens your PFC function, making emotional regulation easier the next day.

2. Cortisol Reduction and Immune Support

Gratitude provides a natural detox for the stress system. The practice actively reduces the levels of **cortisol**, your body's primary stress hormone.

- **The Mechanism:** A state of gratitude activates the parasympathetic nervous system ("rest-and-digest"), shifting resources away from the constant high alert that characterizes chronic stress. This dampening of the stress response directly lowers cortisol levels.

- **The Proof:** Studies connecting gratitude and appreciation found that participants experienced a reduction in cortisol levels and had better cardiac function. This reduction in cortisol is particularly important because high cortisol is often linked to diminished immune function. By lowering cortisol through gratitude, you are actively supporting your immune system and increasing your physiological resilience against chronic ailments.

Gratitude is a behavioral intervention that chemically regulates the negative stress response, building genuine physiological resistance to environmental stress.

Integration with Your Existing Skills

The gratitude journal serves as the practical application lab for all the skills you have learned so far, cementing them into one system:

1. **Reinforcing the HEAL Method (Book 1):** The journaling process is the mandatory second phase of the HEAL method. You use the journal to *Enrich* and *Absorb* the positive experience. By writing the *Why* and *How* of the good feeling, you ensure the positive memory is detailed and robust enough to create lasting neural change.

2. **Counteracting Rumination (Book 2):** The journal forces a shift in your attention's object. Instead of dwelling on past conflicts or future worries (rumination), your mind is constructively focused on the present moment's positive data. This practice, when done consistently, makes it easier for you to interrupt the toxic replay loop when anger strikes.

3. **Fuels Compassion (Book 3):** By focusing on the effort and kind intent of others, the journal strengthens your capacity for compassion. This practice helps you reduce toxic emotions like envy and resentment by forcing a comparative focus on what is good in your life, rather than what is missing in comparison to others.

The commitment to a structured gratitude journal ensures the continuous sensitization of your brain toward positive affect. This simple, evidence-based habit is the engine that drives your inner strength, setting the stage for deeper relational appreciation.

CHAPTER 2
FEEL THE HEALTH BENEFITS: GRATITUDE'S EFFECT ON STRESS AND SLEEP

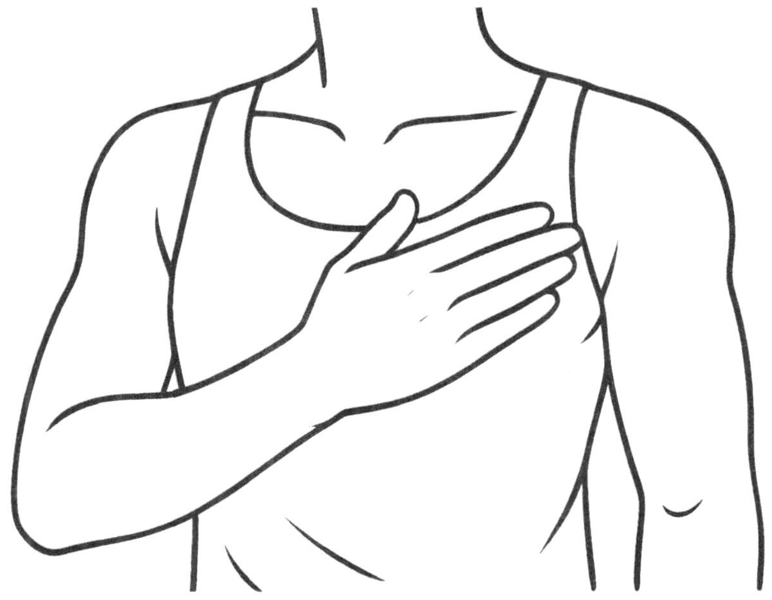

In the previous chapter, you learned how to start your gratitude journal, training your selective attention to consistently register positive data. This cognitive shift, from looking for lack to looking for abundance, is powerful for your mental state.

But the effect of gratitude is not confined to your mind. It is a powerful physiological intervention. The mental habit of appreciation generates measurable, verifiable physical changes in your body, directly addressing the damage caused by chronic stress and anxiety (the initial problem addressed in Book 2).

This chapter provides the scientific evidence for gratitude's physical power. We will explore how consistent gratitude practice detoxifies your stress system by lowering cortisol, strengthens your cardiac function, and, crucially, improves the quality of your sleep. By understanding these deep, physical benefits, you gain confidence that your deliberate effort to cultivate appreciation is a vital part of your long-term health plan.

Chronic negativity and sustained hostility (the habits this entire guide is working to reverse) keep the body in a state of low-level physiological arousal: a continuous sympathetic overdrive. This state is highly damaging, and it is chemically maintained by the stress hormone **cortisol**.

Cortisol is the primary chemical messenger in your body's fight-or-flight response. While essential for immediate danger, chronic, high levels of cortisol are linked to inflammation, weakened immune function, and the negative neuroplasticity that impairs emotional regulation in the brain (Book 1). You cannot achieve sustainable inner strength if your body is constantly flooded with the chemical signal of stress.

Gratitude acts as a direct, natural detox for this system.

- **The Mechanism of Downregulation:** Committing to a daily gratitude practice forces your mind to dwell on feelings of contentment, safety, and sufficiency. This emotional state activates the **parasympathetic nervous system**, your "rest-and-digest" system, shifting resources away from the constant high alert that characterizes chronic stress. This systemic shift directly dampens the HPA (hypothalamic-pituitary-adrenal) axis, which is the system that produces cortisol.

- **The Measurable Proof:** Studies on gratitude and appreciation have found that participants experienced a measurable **reduction in cortisol levels**. This reduction confirms that the deliberate mental habit of appreciation chemically regulates the negative stress response. By lowering cortisol, you are actively supporting your immune system and increasing your physiological resilience against chronic ailments.

This physiological dampening is why gratitude is correlated with resilience. When your cortisol levels are lower, your body is simply better equipped to handle stress. You are more resilient to emotional setbacks and negative experiences, allowing you to approach challenges with more awareness and a broader perspective, rather than collapsing into emotional reaction.

Strengthening the Heart: Cardiac Function and Resilience

The benefits of gratitude extend directly to your cardiovascular system, reinforcing the internal regulation work you mastered in Book 2 (HRV).

Recall that Heart Rate Variability (HRV) is the measure of the healthy fluctuation between heartbeats, and high HRV is strongly associated with better vagal nerve function and superior emotional regulation. Chronic stress and anger are linked to low, rigid HRV, which places the heart under increased workload.

- **The Cardiac Benefit:** Studies found that participants who engaged in structured appreciation experienced **better cardiac function**. This occurs because the sustained, positive emotional state promoted by gratitude encourages rhythmic, slow breathing and engages the parasympathetic system (the vagal brake), which stabilizes heart function.

- **Increased Resilience to Setbacks:** When you practice gratitude, you are essentially training your body to maintain a state of calm balance. This training helps your heart and nervous system cope better with sudden negative input. Gratitude makes you more resilient to emotional setbacks because your body is not starting from a place of high physiological arousal.

This objective evidence means that the practice of appreciating the good in your life is not a luxury; it is a vital, self-administered intervention for maintaining cardiovascular and emotional health. It ensures that the high HRV and low heart rate you achieved through breathing exercises (Book 2) are maintained throughout your daily life.

The Sleep Solution: Breaking the Cycle of Arousal

One of the most immediate and appreciated benefits of gratitude journaling is its profound impact on sleep quality. If you struggle to fall asleep or maintain sleep, the primary culprit is often high **psychological arousal**, the constant, toxic loop of worry and planning that keeps your mind active at night.

- **The Failure of Suppressing Worry:** Trying to simply *force* yourself to stop worrying rarely works, because the anxious thoughts are often fueled by the negative bias and sustained by physiological tension (low HRV, high cortisol).

- **The Gratitude Intervention:** Gratitude provides a functional replacement for worry. By intentionally shifting your focus to three to five specific things you are genuinely appreciative of before you lie down, you force your mind to engage with positive, calming data. This conscious shift interrupts the toxic cycle of planning and rumination that keeps you awake. It redirects your attention away from threats and toward safety and contentment, which are the necessary internal conditions for sleep.

- **The Measurable Proof:** Studies consistently indicate that people who regularly practice gratitude journaling report **better quality sleep** and often fall asleep in a shorter period of time. By soothing a racing heart and calming the nervous system, gratitude acts as a natural relaxant, allowing your body to transition smoothly into a regenerative state. Better sleep, in turn, strengthens your Prefrontal Cortex (PFC), enhancing your emotional regulation and memory the next day.

Gratitude is thus a direct behavioral remedy for the stress-induced sleep disruption that characterizes high-pressure modern life.

The Mechanism of Deep Focus: From Superficial to Enduring

The power of gratitude to induce these health benefits depends on the intensity and duration of your focus. Simply thinking a quick thank you is a good start, but it does not generate lasting chemical change. You must commit to **savoring** the experience.

This chapter reinforces the principles of the **HEAL Method** (Book 1, Chapter 4), emphasizing the importance of *Enriching* and *Absorbing* the feeling for at least 15 to 30 seconds. When journaling, this means going deep into the *how* and *why* of the feeling:

- **The Cognitive Detail:** Why did the conversation feel good? (Because my colleague validated my idea.)
- **The Emotional Detail:** What specific emotion did that trigger? (Pride, competence, ease.)
- **The Somatic Detail:** Where did I feel it in my body? (Warmth in the chest, relaxation in the jaw.)

This sustained, detailed focus on positive affect is what facilitates the neuroplastic change that lowers your body's stress threshold. It is this depth of engagement that makes gratitude a functional tool for physiological health.

Gratitude as Internal Fortitude

This chapter confirms that the daily habit of gratitude journaling is not a soft suggestion; it is a critical intervention for maintaining your physical and emotional equilibrium. It actively detoxifies the chemical residue of past negativity and hostility.

By consistently integrating journaling, you are lowering your cortisol levels, improving your cardiac resilience, and guaranteeing better sleep. This foundation of internal fortitude ensures that the emotional strength you have built is resilient, reliable, and deeply wired. You are moving from relying on external circumstances for happiness to generating inner strength through your own intentional focus.

The next step is to take this deep internal resource and apply it to your most important relationships. We move now from the solitary act of journaling to the powerful, bonding act of written appreciation.

CHAPTER 3

GO DEEPER: USING WRITTEN APPRECIATION TO STRENGTHEN BONDS

You have achieved consistency. You know the gratitude journal is working its quiet magic, lowering your stress, improving your sleep, and training your attention to find the good. That internal work is essential. It is the steady income of emotional resilience.

But here is the truth about human connection: we are not built to thrive in isolation. We are deeply social creatures. The highest form of gratitude, the practice that generates the most durable, life-altering change, is not solitary. It is **relational**.

When your appreciation shifts from a simple list in a journal to a structured piece of written appreciation addressed to another human being, the impact multiplies. This focused practice, often called a gratitude letter, is a high-leverage emotional action. It targets and strengthens the specific social bonds that support your life. Research confirms this targeted practice generates more intense benefits and longer-lasting effects than journaling alone. You are not just being kind. You are actively repairing and reinforcing the very social fabric that sustains your emotional health.

Why is writing a letter more powerful than a journal entry? It is about activation.

Your daily journal helps you manage the negativity bias inside your head. The letter forces you to process the good experience through the lens of *another person's agency* and *effort*. This is a massive cognitive leap. It activates stronger **social cognition processes** in your brain.

The emotional reward is intensified because you are engaging in the full reward circuit related to connection and prosocial behavior.

1. **Activating Social Pathways:** When you write a letter detailing how someone's effort helped you, you engage the neural pathways responsible for complex social behavior, including the areas linked to empathy and "theory of mind" (mPFC and dlPFC, as discussed in Book 3). You are actively thinking about their intentions, their effort, and the cost they incurred to help you.

2. **Durable Neuroplastic Change:** This targeted relational focus creates more robust and durable neural changes. It reinforces the brain's social pathways and the reward circuits associated with prosocial behavior, making the feeling of connection itself more valuable and lasting. The benefits, including sustained improvements in mood and life satisfaction, are often reported weeks and months after the letter is written and delivered.

3. **Overcoming Emotional Debt:** The negativity bias often creates emotional debt in relationships. We quickly absorb criticism or perceived slights (the cost) but fail to register or vocalize appreciation (the reward). This creates an unbalanced emotional ledger. The gratitude letter is a specific, powerful action that clears that debt, transforming a relationship from one of potential deficit to one of clear abundance.

The letter is not just a nice gesture. It is a strategically deployed tool designed to generate and solidify emotional resilience through confirmed social connection.

The Protocol: Structuring Your Appreciation Letter

A letter only achieves these powerful benefits if it moves beyond vague compliments. It must convey genuine, specific appreciation. The goal is to make the recipient feel seen, valued, and understood at a deep, relational level.

The writing protocol involves three essential components that directly link the action back to the principles of NVC (Book 3) and the HEAL Method (Book 1).

1. Identify the Specific Contribution (The Observation)

You must start with verifiable facts, just like in NVC's **Observation** step. Identify a specific action, event, date, or quality of the person that profoundly impacted you. You must move past generic praise (e.g., "You are a kind person") to the specific, tangible evidence of their kindness.

- **Focus:** Be precise about the "when" and "what." Detail the moment so the recipient cannot doubt that you were paying attention.

- *Ineffective:* "Thank you for all your support over the years."

- *Effective:* "I am writing specifically about the Tuesday two months ago when I was completely swamped with the Smith account. You saw me panic, and without being asked, you took the lead on the client call, taking all the pressure off me."

This specificity is critical. It proves you were not just passively benefiting from their kindness. You were actively noticing their effort, which is a major reward in any relationship (Social Exchange Theory).

2. Describe the Emotional and Practical Impact (The Feeling and Need)

This is the emotional core of the letter. You must articulate the internal emotional impact their specific action had on you, linking it to a core, universal need that was met. This requires honest vulnerability.

- **Action Focus:** Describe the "before and after." What negative feeling did they help alleviate (e.g., fear, loneliness, panic), and what positive feeling did they create (e.g., safety, competence, peace)? This engages the listener's empathy.

- *Ineffective:* "That was a big help."

- *Effective:* "Before you stepped in on that call, I was feeling totally overwhelmed and panicked, which was violating my deep need for **professional competence** and **safety** in my job. Your action immediately met those needs. It gave me a sense of calm and competence back, which allowed me to think clearly and finish the project correctly."

This deep articulation moves the appreciation from a surface level to a profound human connection. The recipient understands their effort had a quantifiable, positive effect on your well-being, which is intrinsically rewarding (reward circuits, Book 3, Chapter 5).

3. Express Profound Thanks and Future Intent (The Commitment)

Conclude the letter by summarizing the lasting value of their action and, if appropriate, state your commitment to maintaining the bond.

- **Action Focus:** Reiterate the long-term emotional or practical resource their kindness created.
- *Effective:* "Thank you. That moment of support was not just a one-time favor; it built my confidence to handle the next crisis. Knowing I can rely on your partnership is something I deeply value. I commit to being there for you with the same calm and focus whenever you need it."

The Durable Benefits of Relational Gratitude

The sustained effects of gratitude letters validate their power as a superior tool for emotional strengthening.

- **Sustained Emotional Boost:** The positive emotions generated are not fleeting. Participants report measurable improvements in overall mood, life satisfaction, and interpersonal relationships for **weeks and months** after completing gratitude letter exercises. This durability proves that the practice creates lasting neural changes, building genuine emotional resilience, rather than merely temporary emotional states.
- **Reduced Toxic Comparison:** By intentionally focusing on the benevolence and positive intentions of others, the practice of writing appreciation letters actively counters toxic emotions like envy and resentment. You train your mind to look for connection and good intent, rather than focusing on the deficits that comparison (envy) creates.
- **Health and Coping Outcomes:** This relational gratitude supports the physiological benefits noted in Chapter 3: continued reduction in stress hormones (cortisol) and increased resilience against emotional setbacks, which is linked to better cardiac function. You use the power of connection to chemically regulate your body.

The Reciprocal Loop: Find-Remind-Bind Theory

The delivery of your written appreciation does more than just make the recipient feel good. It activates a powerful **reciprocal loop** that strengthens your entire social network. This loop is explained by the **Find-Remind-Bind Theory** of gratitude.

1. **Find:** Gratitude helps the giver *find* and recognize others who are valuable and worthy of sustained social connection (i.e., people who consistently provide support and kindness).

2. **Remind:** The explicit expression of gratitude *reminds* the recipient of their own prosocial behavior. This act is intrinsically rewarding and motivates them to continue acting kindly toward the grateful person ("I want to do this again").

3. **Bind:** The reciprocal cycle *binds* the two individuals together, deepening the social bonds and motivating both parties to seek continued connection.

This cycle means the inner strength you gain from gratitude directly increases your prosocial motivation, your desire to help and share with others, which is a key component of emotional health and social acceptance. By reinforcing the goodness received, you are cognitively and chemically motivated to contribute goodness back to the social exchange.

Action Plan: Moving from Journaling to Letters

Your task is to choose at least one person this week who has made a specific, positive impact and write them a structured letter of appreciation.

Step 1: Select the Target: Choose someone whose effort you have not fully acknowledged.

Step 2: Draft the Three-Part Script: Use the protocol outlined above to ensure your letter is specific, emotionally vulnerable, and committed to future connection.

Step 3: Deliver and Observe the Reward: The final step is delivering the letter, preferably in person, if possible. After the delivery, pause and reflect on the resulting feeling. This moment, the visible confirmation that your effort strengthened a valued bond, is the most potent reward. It is this relational feedback that cements the positive neuroplastic change more powerfully than a solitary journal entry.

By integrating written appreciation into your habits, you are using high-leverage emotional action to rewire your social brain. You are transforming passive observation into an active engine for connection, ensuring that your inner strength is constantly reinforced by the quality of your relationships.

CHAPTER 4
EXPAND YOUR FOCUS:
GRATITUDE FOR RESILIENCE AND HARD TIMES

You have successfully used gratitude to deepen your internal quiet. You are training your attention daily through journaling, and you have experienced the profound bonding power of written appreciation (Chapter 4). You know gratitude works when things are simply okay.

But life is not always okay.

Inevitably, genuine stress returns. You face a major financial reversal, a sudden conflict, or a serious professional setback. When these crises hit, the negativity bias screams loudest, threatening to hijack all the calm and clarity you have achieved. Your mind reverts to focusing on loss, risk, and lack.

The purpose of this chapter is to prepare you for that moment. We must ensure that your commitment to gratitude is not merely a fair-weather habit but a core psychological muscle that fires fastest under pressure. Gratitude, applied intentionally during genuine adversity, is your most powerful tool for building **resilience**, the ability to adapt and recover quickly from hardship. It prevents your mind from collapsing into toxic comparison and sustained despair.

Resilience is not about being tough or ignoring pain. It is about the efficiency and speed with which you can restore your body and mind to equilibrium after a shock. Without gratitude, the mind defaults to two deeply corrosive behaviors during a crisis:

1. The Collapse into Envy and Comparison

When suffering a setback, a job loss, a divorce, an illness, the mind has a dangerous knack for immediately comparing your life to a perceived ideal or to the apparent success of others. This comparison activates the toxic emotions of envy, jealousy, and resentment.

- **The Mechanism of Envy:** Envy is focusing on what is *missing* in your life relative to someone else's perceived abundance. If you are struggling financially, your mind finds every person enjoying ease. If you are facing relational trouble, your mind fixes on couples who seem happy. This comparison creates a sense of profound injustice and inadequacy, which is entirely self-defeating.

- **The Cost:** Envy consumes vast mental bandwidth, trapping you in a cycle of dissatisfaction and robbing you of the energy needed for practical problem-solving. It ensures that the emotional focus is entirely on *deficits* and *lack*, which reinforces the negativity bias.

2. The Mental Filter of Loss

During genuine hard times, the cognitive distortion known as the **Mental Filter** (Book 1) becomes intensely destructive. Your mind becomes hyper-focused on the specific loss, the health problem, the failed investment, the hurtful remark, while actively filtering out all the resources, support systems, and good things that remain present in your life.

This failure to see the full, balanced picture is what causes feelings of hopelessness. The world appears entirely dark because your mental filter is temporarily blocking out the light.

Gratitude is the direct, intentional counter-measure to both of these states. It forces the mind to shift its gaze from the *gap* (what is lost) to the *ground* (what remains, what is sufficient, and what is currently supporting you).

The practice of gratitude builds genuine internal fortitude by changing how you process difficult information. It does not deny the pain of the setback; it places the pain within a broader context of resources and support.

Studies show a strong correlation between feeling grateful and experiencing greater resilience and emotional strength. This happens because gratitude actively trains the mind to cope with difficult circumstances by adopting a **broader perception** and increased awareness of surrounding factors.

1. Focusing on the "What Remains"

When facing loss, your immediate instinct is to list what is gone. Gratitude forces you to list what is *still present* and functional.

- *Scenario*: You lose a significant project or client (financial loss).
- *Default Negative Focus:* "I lost the client. I am a failure. My finances are ruined." (Catastrophizing, Mental Filter).
- *Gratitude Resilience Focus:* "The loss is painful, but what remains? I still have my core professional competence. I still have a positive relationship with my past clients. I still have my health and my network. I still have two months of savings. I appreciate the financial security I built that allows me to withstand this setback."

This conscious reframing shifts your attention from the destructive thought of "ruin" to the constructive action of "resources." It affirms that the integrity of your life is defined by the whole picture, not one missing piece.

2. Maintaining Stress Tolerance

During a crisis, the body's natural response is to flood the system with cortisol and adrenaline. This keeps you in a debilitating state of high arousal. Resilience is measured by how effectively you can regulate this flood, preventing it from spiraling into anxiety or aggressive reaction (Book 2).

- **The Chemical Buffer:** Gratitude acts as a continuous emotional buffer. By maintaining a grateful state, even for small things, you continue to activate the parasympathetic nervous system, which helps lower the baseline levels of cortisol. This physiological dampening ensures that when the crisis hits, your stress system is not starting from an already hyper-aroused state.

- **The Proof:** Research has specifically shown that participants who experienced a reduction in stress hormones (cortisol) and exhibited better cardiac function were also more resilient to emotional setbacks and negative experiences. This underscores that gratitude is not just mental wishful thinking. It provides a real, chemical shield against the damaging effects of external stress.

By practicing gratitude in hard times, you are actively choosing to protect your body's stress tolerance threshold, ensuring that you can think clearly enough to engage your problem-solving skills (Book 2, Chapter 5) rather than collapsing into emotional paralysis.

Applying Gratitude in Crisis: The Reframing Lens

To maximize gratitude's impact during adversity, you need specific, high-leverage practices that directly challenge the "Mental Filter" and the "All-or-Nothing Thinking" (Book 1, Chapter 2) that thrive in crisis.

Action Tool 1: The "This is Tolerable" Practice

When the pressure is overwhelming, the mind often defaults to the catastrophic belief that the current suffering is unbearable. The "This is Tolerable" Practice forces an acceptance of the present reality while acknowledging the small things that prevent total collapse.

1. **Acknowledge the Pain (Fact):** State the difficulty directly without minimizing it. *Example: "I am feeling deep anxiety about my finances."*

2. **Identify the Tolerable Present:** Immediately shift attention to the small, objective facts that are *currently* making the situation non-terminal.

   - *Example Focus:* "I am breathing easily right now. I have a roof over my head tonight. I have food in the refrigerator. My physical body is not in immediate danger. The current moment is **tolerable**."

3. **Find Gratitude in the Unseen Support:** Express appreciation for the often-unseen infrastructure that keeps the crisis from becoming a total catastrophe. *Example: "I appreciate the consistent effort of my partner who is working hard, and I am grateful for the structural security of our home."*

This practice grounds you firmly in the present moment, which is a known benefit of expressing gratitude. It pulls your focus away from the speculative, catastrophic future and into the factual, manageable present, enabling you to conserve your energy for real problem-solving.

Action Tool 2: Gratitude for the "Dark Teacher"

This advanced application involves finding appreciation not just *despite* the adversity, but sometimes *for* the adversity itself, viewing it as a "Dark Teacher" or a catalyst for growth. This is the ultimate expression of resilience.

- **The Focus:** You are not grateful *for* the suffering, but grateful *for the clarity or competence* the suffering forced you to develop.
- *Scenario:* A relational conflict that was painful but necessary (Book 3).
- *Gratitude Focus:* "I am grateful that the conflict forced us to finally use the DESC Script and define our boundaries (Chapter 3). Before the fight, we never had the courage to set these limits. I appreciate the **clarity** and **strength** that the pain delivered."

This form of gratitude helps you transform the energy of failure or loss into the energy of learning and growth. It is a powerful form of cognitive restructuring, actively replacing the sense of helplessness with a sense of growth and agency. The consistent practice of this perspective is what allows people to cope with difficult circumstances with a broader, more resourceful mindset.

The Role of Relational Gratitude in Crisis

When under acute stress, the tendency is to isolate, withdrawing from others to manage shame or fear. This isolation is dangerous because it removes the very social support systems that buffer stress and promote prosocial behavior.

This is where the relational practices from Chapter 4 become vital.

- **Reinforcing the Bond:** When you are struggling, expressing gratitude to those who are helping you, even for small efforts, reinforces the **reciprocal loop** (Find-Remind-Bind Theory). You remind the helper that their effort is seen and valued, which motivates them to continue providing support. This is critical for stabilizing the social exchange during a high-cost period.

- **The Strength of Connection:** Expressing gratitude, even when you feel depleted, encourages prosocial behavior and increases the desire to spend time with others, countering the isolation driven by anxiety. Social support is crucial for mitigating the negative emotional effects of stress, anxiety, and loneliness.

The consistent practice of relational gratitude, even if it is just a text message appreciating a friend's patience, ensures that your lifeline remains intact during the storm.

The Unwavering Inner Strength

The practices in this chapter, focusing on what remains, auditing for tolerance, and reframing adversity, ensure that gratitude moves from a simple feeling to an **unwavering inner strength**.

This strength is quantifiable: you are chemically regulating your stress response, emotionally counteracting toxic comparison, and cognitively maintaining a broad, solution-oriented perspective, even when the pressure is immense.

By committing to gratitude, you are seizing control of your emotional destiny by ensuring your focus is on abundance, not lack. This final, integrated practice is the most powerful tool for maintaining your resilient outlook, preparing you for the final book, where we will translate this inner strength into the external integrity of self-respect and clear boundaries.

CHAPTER 5

GIVE IT BACK: GRATITUDE AND INCREASING PROSOCIAL BEHAVIOR

You have done the deep work. You have trained your mind to find the good, to appreciate the specific efforts of others, and to use that focus to calm your body and lower your stress hormones. You have built a serious, durable internal reserve of emotional resilience.

But what is inner strength for, if not to be spent?

If you keep that abundance bottled up, it stagnates. The greatest function of gratitude is relational: it serves as the most reliable indicator that you are ready to engage in **prosocial behavior**, the actions intended to help, share, and cooperate with others. When you feel genuinely grateful, you are chemically and cognitively motivated to contribute kindness back into the social world, completing a powerful, positive feedback loop that stabilizes your relationships and reinforces your own peace.

This commitment to external generosity is the final step in this book. It ensures that your kind speech (Book 3) is consistently backed by generous action. We are translating inner appreciation into external momentum.

Why Kindness is Not Optional: The Prosocial Mandate

Prosocial behaviors are simply actions intended to help other people, driven by a fundamental concern for their feelings and welfare. Holding a door open, sharing a resource, offering comfort, or cooperating are all part of this. They are the behavioral opposite of the hurtful and hostile habits you are discarding.

Why must you make this a priority? Because kind action is necessary for the health of your social life and your own mental state:

1. **The Social Glue:** Prosocial actions forge connections and hold the fabric of social life together. They help you establish social support, which is critical for coping with personal hardships. When you are kind, you build the safety net you will inevitably need.

2. **The Mood-Boosting Effect:** Kindness is its own reward system. Research has consistently shown that people who frequently engage in prosocial behaviors are more likely to experience better moods. It gets better: people who help others tend to experience negative moods *less frequently*. Helping is an active way to keep the negativity bias at bay (Book 1).

3. **Stress Management:** Need a reliable way to reduce the impact of stress? Help someone else. Research found that engaging in prosocial behaviors helps mitigate the negative emotional effects of stress on the helper. When you focus outward to assist another person, you constructively redirect cognitive energy away from your internal worries, giving your mind a functional, positive task.

You are not being asked to be a martyr. You are being asked to engage in an action that is scientifically proven to improve your own mood, reduce your stress, and solidify your social safety net.

The Reciprocal Engine: Find-Remind-Bind Theory

How exactly does feeling grateful (an internal state) lead to a powerful motivation to act (an external state)? The **Find-Remind-Bind Theory** provides the scientific roadmap for this reciprocal cycle. This theory confirms that expressing thanks is not the conclusion of the process; it is the catalyst for the next round of connection.

1. **Find:** Gratitude first helps the individual *find* and recognize others who are valuable and worthy of sustained social connection, those who reliably provide support and kindness. You sharpen your social intelligence by prioritizing healthy, supportive relationships.

2. **Remind:** The expression of gratitude, whether through a quick text or a detailed letter (Chapter 4), *reminds* the recipient of their own prosocial behavior. This act is intrinsically rewarding to the helper and motivates them to continue acting kindly toward the grateful person. Your thanks acts as positive reinforcement for their generosity.

3. **Bind:** The resulting reciprocal cycle *binds* the two individuals together, strengthening the social bond. This deepens the relationship and motivates both parties to seek continued connection, stabilizing the social exchange.

This entire mechanism confirms that gratitude is a powerful, direct predictor of prosocial motivation. By acknowledging the support you receive, you are chemically and cognitively motivated to repay that kindness, creating a durable, positive loop in your social exchanges. Your inner strength is literally multiplied by the strength of your connections.

Action Tool 1: The Daily Kindness Commitment

To actively engage this reciprocal cycle, you must integrate small, low-cost acts of kindness into your daily routine. This turns your internal appreciation into external momentum. This principle is supported by research showing that prompting individuals to engage in kind acts yields benefits beyond personal happiness, promoting better social acceptance and overall well-being.

Action Focus: Proactive, Measurable Kindness

The act must be low-cost and easily achievable. This leverages the **SMART goal** principles you mastered in Book 1 (Chapter 5), guaranteeing a successful win that reinforces your motivation (dopamine release).

1. **Verbal Validation:** Commit to giving one sincere, specific compliment or verbal validation today. The focus must be on **effort or competence**, not just appearance. Don't be vague. *Example: Instead of saying, "Your presentation was fine," say, "I really appreciated the specific effort you put into structuring that opening section; the way you handled the data made the entire complex argument immediately clear."* This uses your Kind Speech skills

(Book 3) to deliver a clear, high-reward message that reinforces their competence.

2. **Removing a Burden:** Look for a small burden you can quietly remove from someone else's path, especially in a shared environment. *Example: Without being asked, take out a communal recycling bin, or silently wipe down the shared kitchen counter at work.* This small, unsolicited act of support reinforces the social bond by demonstrating attention and care, fulfilling the other person's need for **ease** and **support** (NVC, Book 3).

3. **Offer Presence:** Intentionally set aside your phone and offer a few minutes of **undivided attention** to someone who is speaking to you. *Example: Fully listen to a colleague or partner recount a stressful event without interrupting, distracting yourself, or formulating your own response.* This fulfills the basic human need for presence, validation, and being truly heard, which is a powerful prosocial act that mitigates their stress.

These actions are deliberate attempts to inject positive rewards into your social environment, ensuring your relationships are defined by mutual support and abundance.

Action Tool 2: Gratitude as a Strategy Against Envy

Prosocial behavior is not just about doing favors. It is a powerful psychological strategy for managing complex internal emotional dynamics, specifically those related to toxic comparison and material scarcity (Book 4, Chapter 5).

When you feel that sharp twinge of envy regarding another person's success, a big promotion, a new piece of property, or effortless ease, your mind is locked on focusing on *lack* and *injustice*. This internal state often leads to passive-aggressive behavior or hostility toward the person you envy, damaging the relationship. Gratitude provides a functional alternative.

Action Focus: Appreciating the Process, Not the Outcome

1. **Acknowledge the Pain (Fact):** State the feeling without judgment: "I feel a sharp twinge of envy when I see my colleague's new leadership title."

2. **Shift to Process Gratitude:** Immediately shift your focus to appreciating the *process, effort,* or *competence* that person likely invested to achieve that goal. You must engage your Empathy Circuits (Book 3) to see their struggle. *Example: "I appreciate the*

consistent dedication and early mornings my colleague clearly exerted over the last year to master those skills. I am grateful for their visible example of competence and hard work; it shows what is possible."

3. **Translate to Self-Action:** Convert that appreciation into a positive, low-cost action for yourself. This turns envy into motivation. *Example: "I will immediately send them a congratulatory note (prosocial behavior), and then I will use the next hour to work on my own SMART goal for professional skill development (Book 1, Chapter 5)."*

By appreciating their process, you transform the toxic energy of envy into the functional energy of motivation and prosocial action. This prevents the corrosive effects of envy from damaging your relationships, fulfilling your personal value of *integrity* by aligning your actions with your best self.

Integrating External Action with Internal Strength

The practices in this chapter ensure that your external actions reinforce the deep internal strength you have built across all four books.

- **Fuels Kind Speech (Book 3):** Your mastery of assertive communication is strongest when it comes from a place of gratitude and generosity, not demand. Gratitude for a reliable partner makes it easier to use the DESC script with care and acceptance when addressing a conflict, rather than reverting to criticism and aggression. The emotional reserve provided by gratitude (low cortisol, high positive affect) acts as a buffer, ensuring your assertive requests are delivered with the respect that makes them effective.

- **Reinforces Integrity (Book 5):** Living a life of integrity requires aligning your actions with your core values (Book 5, Chapter 6). If your values include "kindness," "community," or "support," then the consistent practice of prosocial behavior ensures that your external actions align with your internal principles. This alignment is the highest form of self-respect.

- **Combats Hostility (Book 2):** Prosocial commitment provides a healthy, positive outlet for emotional energy, preventing the accumulation of resentment and stress that often fuels aggressive outbursts. Helping others mitigates the negative emotional effects of your own stress.

The inner strength you have built through gratitude is now your engine for kindness. By moving from internal appreciation to external, measurable action, you are contributing to a positive, resilient social exchange that supports your well-being and strengthens your connections. This commitment to prosocial action is the final step before we focus on the external integrity of self-respect and boundaries.

CONCLUSION

THE GRATITUDE HABIT: MAINTAINING YOUR NEW OUTLOOK AND HEALTH

You have arrived at a significant turning point. This book was your training camp for emotional self-sufficiency. You took the idea of being thankful and turned it into a structured, daily habit. You now know that genuine gratitude is not just a nice feeling you wait for. It is a powerful, active tool you generate and control.

We must conclude with a clear understanding: the emotional quiet you feel now is not luck. It is the direct, measurable result of consistent effort. You have ensured that the strength you built is reliable, verifiable, and self-sustaining. This is how you make an outlook based on abundance, not scarcity, your new, permanent way of life.

The Science of Proof: You Are Resilient

The greatest reward for mastering gratitude is the objective proof that your internal systems are repairing. You are seeing a quantifiable decrease in the negative chemistry that defined your past habits.

1. Measurable Relief from Worry and Despair

The emotional toll of constant negativity and hostility is immense. You tackled this burden head-on. The systematic work you did, forcing your mind to track positive data daily through journaling, has provided clinical relief you can trust.

- **Anxiety Reduction:** It is not a small thing. Studies confirm that people who consistently used gratitude interventions experienced a significant reduction in anxiety symptoms. This shows up as a **7.76% lower score on the Generalized Anxiety Disorder (GAD-7) assessment** compared to control groups. That drop in anxiety is your freedom. It proves that your mind is now less consumed by the pervasive "what-if" scenarios that previously paralyzed you.

- **Depression Relief:** Similarly, the same analysis found that gratitude interventions led to a significant reduction in depressive symptoms, achieving a **6.89% lower score on the Patient Health Questionnaire-9 (PHQ-9)**. This proves that the daily, deliberate focus on what is present and functional actively counteracts the sense of hopelessness and deficit that fuels depression. Gratitude forces your mind to find evidence of sufficiency, which is the direct cognitive antidote to despair.

This objective evidence means your mind is quieter and less prone to worry and negative rumination. It is a functional success.

2. Physiological Regulation and Resilience

Your gratitude practice has become a powerful, continuous maintenance program for your physical health and the calm you mastered in Book 2.

- **Cortisol Detox:** Chronic stress, the foundation of negative habits, is chemically maintained by the stress hormone, **cortisol.** By consistently dwelling on feelings of safety and contentment through journaling and savoring, you activated the parasympathetic nervous system (the brake). This behavioral choice leads to a measurable **reduction in cortisol levels**. This reduction is vital because lowered cortisol supports immune function and actively counteracts the negative neuroplasticity that impairs emotional regulation in the PFC (Book 1).

- **Improved Cardiac Function and Resilience:** Studies indicate that the sustained emotional state promoted by gratitude is linked to **better cardiac function** and measurable resilience against emotional setbacks. When your body is regulated by gratitude, it is quicker to adapt and recover from stress.

- **Sleep Quality:** The intentional shift in attention before bedtime allows you to successfully interrupt the psychological arousal that causes insomnia and rumination (Book 2). Studies consistently confirm that people who practice gratitude journaling report **better quality sleep**. This improved sleep, in turn, strengthens the regulatory power of your Prefrontal Cortex (PFC), enhancing your emotional control and memory capacity the following day.

You are now physically, chemically, and neurologically more resilient to the pressures of the external world because your internal focus is on sufficiency and safety.

The Sustained Mechanism: Making the Good Stick

The durability of these changes relies on your mastery of neuroplastic principles: sensitization and savoring. You have successfully taught your brain to prioritize the positive.

1. **Creating "Velcro for the Good":** Your brain operates on sensitization: repeated activation makes neural circuits more responsive. You spent this book using your **Gratitude Journal** and the **HEAL Method** (Book 1) to force your mind to focus intently on the good for extended periods (savoring). This sustained focus is what facilitates neuroplastic change, ensuring that your brain becomes faster and more efficient at registering and holding onto positive input (the "Velcro for the good").

2. **Relational Reinforcement:** The practice of **Written Appreciation** (Chapter 4) further cemented this change by reinforcing your **social cognition** circuits. By consistently acknowledging the efforts of others, you tapped into the highly rewarding reciprocal loop (**Find-Remind-Bind Theory**, Chapter 6). When you express gratitude, the recipient is motivated to continue their prosocial behavior, and you are motivated to sustain the grateful habit because you receive the reward of reinforced connection. This social reinforcement makes the habit of gratitude intrinsically self-sustaining.

3. **Countering Toxic Emotions:** This consistent, active focus on abundance ensures that you move beyond the toxic cycle of **envy and comparison** that destroys self-worth (Chapter 5). By

consciously focusing on the *assets* and *competence* you possess and the *resources* that surround you, you build a powerful cognitive shield against the internal pressure of perceived lack.

Integrating Gratitude for Lifelong Maintenance

The inner strength you have built is now the non-negotiable emotional resource that stabilizes and fuels the entire five-book system.

- **Fuels Kind Speech and Assertiveness (Book 3):** Your mastery of assertive communication is now delivered from a place of emotional sufficiency, not neediness. Gratitude provides the generous emotional reserve that allows you to be clear and firm (assertive) without becoming demanding or aggressive. You can approach conflict (DESC Script) from a position of "I have plenty, but this is my need," rather than "I need you to fill my empty tank."

- **Supports Agency (Book 1):** Gratitude directly counteracts the feeling of **learned helplessness** (Book 1, Chapter 5). When you face a large problem, your gratitude practice ensures your mind automatically focuses on the **assets** you possess (your health, your network, your skills) rather than the perceived deficit. This shift from focusing on *loss* to focusing on *resources* enables you to launch a strong, solution-oriented action plan.

- **Increases Integrity (Book 5):** When you consistently engage in prosocial behavior (Chapter 6), driven by your gratitude, your external actions align with your internal values of generosity and kindness. This integrity is the highest form of self-respect, and it is the key to setting clear, confident boundaries. The individual who feels abundant is the one who can confidently say "no" when necessary.

The consistency of your daily gratitude practice is now the primary factor in maintaining your positive outlook and health. It is the engine that generates the necessary emotional momentum to keep the entire system running smoothly, ensuring that your emotional state is resilient, reliable, and fundamentally optimistic.

You have secured the internal foundation for a life of emotional clarity. Now, we translate this profound inner strength into the external competence of defining your worth and setting healthy limits.

REFLECTION QUESTIONS

Prosocial behaviour

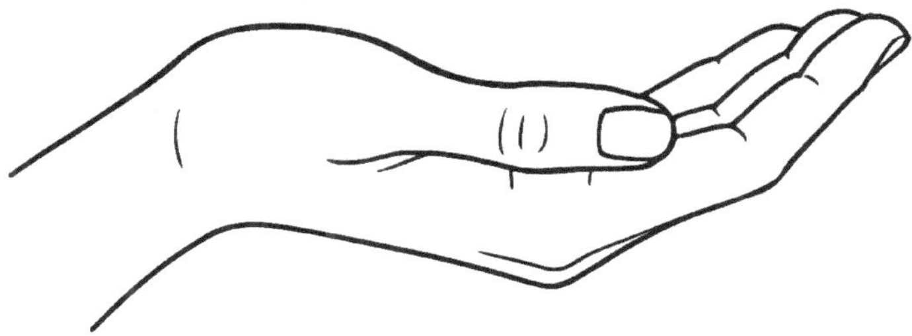

1. Think about your sleep this past week. Did you fall asleep faster or feel more rested? Describe one specific, measurable physical health metric (e.g., time to fall asleep, a subjective score of morning stress) that has improved since starting your evidence-based gratitude journal. How do you quantify this change?

2. Tell me about a time this week where you felt that familiar impulse toward **envy or toxic comparison**. How did you deliberately apply the resilience technique of focusing on "what remains" (Chapter 5) to shift your perspective and conserve energy?

3. Recall one successful **Accountable Apology** or assertive request you made this week (Book 3). How did the emotional reserve and acceptance you cultivated through gratitude make that difficult conversation easier to start and maintain?

4. What was one act of low-cost, proactive **prosocial behavior** (Chapter 6) you engaged in this week? How did the resulting feeling of connection or competence compare to a purely internal journal entry?

5. Look at your journal. Describe a recent entry that went beyond a simple list of objects. Describe the specific, detailed focus you used (What, Why, and How) to successfully *Enrich* and *Absorb* that positive experience. What durable feeling did it leave you with?

BOOK FIVE

DEFINE YOUR SPACE:
PRACTICAL ACTIONS TO SPREAD RESPECT

INTRODUCTION

RESPECT IS RECIPROCITY:
THE FOUNDATION OF HEALTHY RELATIONSHIPS

Congratulations. You made it to the final stage. You achieved profound internal change: you silenced the inner critic (Book 1), you mastered physical and emotional control (Book 2), you learned to speak with clear kindness (Book 3), and you fortified your inner strength with sustained gratitude (Book 4).

But here is where the work gets real. All that hard-won internal peace, that calm, that self-worth, is fragile if you do not protect it. If you fail to define your space, if you do not set and enforce clear personal limits, every resource you built will be systematically drained by others. Your patience will be exhausted by people who chronically disrespect your time, and your energy will be depleted by demands you feel too weak to refuse.

The essential truth of sustaining a positive life is that internal strength must translate into external integrity. The skill that makes this possible is **respect**. We must understand respect not as a soft, abstract ideal, but as a practical, predictable principle that governs all human interaction. We define respect as **reciprocity**, the balanced, mutual regard that ensures every relationship provides equitable value. This book provides the direct, actionable frameworks to establish that balance permanently.

The Problem Defined: The High Cost of the Unbalanced Exchange

Chronic rudeness, hostility, and disrespect are not random character flaws; they are the primary indicators that a relationship system is broken. The science that explains this failure is **Social Exchange Theory (SET)**.

SET is a psychological and sociological framework that posits that all social behavior, from a quick work email to a decades-long marriage, results from a continuous, if often subconscious, calculation. Individuals engage in interaction by weighing the potential **rewards** they receive against the **costs** they incur in that relationship. We choose and maintain relationships that maximize personal benefits and minimize personal disadvantages.

In this framework, respect is the ultimate reward.

- **Rewards** include validation, clear communication, emotional security, shared time, and support (all skills you mastered in Book 3 and 4).
- **Costs** include stress, time wastage, emotional dumping, energy depletion, and, critically, consistent **disrespect** or **rudeness**.

When you consistently engage with hostile habits, negativity, aggression, or a refusal to honor time, you impose a high cost on the other person. SET suggests that people will typically diminish or end a relationship if the **costs consistently outweigh the rewards**, especially if their efforts are not returned.

The Failure of Inequity: Why Relationships Break

Hostile and negative habits destroy relationships by creating **inequity**. Inequity occurs when one person perceives that their effort, time, and emotional investment are not being reciprocated, making the exchange feel unbalanced. This imbalance is where resentment takes root.

The failure to define your space, the collapse into passive compliance or the explosive reaction of aggression, is always a failure to manage this balance.

1. **The Passive Cost Accumulation:** If you default to passive behavior (Book 3, Chapter 3), you allow others to routinely impose costs on you: taking too much of your time, demanding emotional labor, or ignoring your stated needs. When you fail to state your needs, you are teaching the other person that they can safely ignore your wants. This lack of self-respect accumulates internally as resentment, which is repressed anger. This drives up your personal cost until the relationship is no longer tolerable.

2. **The Aggressive Cost Imposition:** Conversely, if you react aggressively, you impose extreme emotional costs on the other person (fear, humiliation, defensiveness). While aggression may achieve short-term compliance, the long-term relational cost is devastating, destroying mutual trust and ensuring the person will eventually withdraw or retaliate.

The path to spreading respect begins with an honest audit of your own relational ledger. You must identify where you are allowing costs to accumulate unchecked and where you are inadvertently imposing unfair costs on others. The functional solution is to establish yourself as a high-value partner in social exchange, one who gives respect generously, but who requires it to be reciprocated predictably.

The Foundation of Boundaries: Protecting Your Mental Health

The practical action for defining your value and ensuring reciprocity is **boundary setting**.

A boundary is simply a limit you identify for yourself and apply through clear communication or deliberate action. Boundaries are not tools for controlling others; they are declarations of self-care necessary to maintain security and health in all relationships, at work and at home.

Setting healthy boundaries is not optional; it is a critical component of maintaining the emotional stability you built in Books 1 and 2.

- **Preventing Burnout and Depletion:** Establishing clear boundaries, especially between your work life and personal life (workplace boundaries), is a proven self-care practice that actively reduces the risk of **workplace burnout**. Warning signs that your boundaries are weak include chronic energy depletion, feelings of negativism related to work, and increased mental distance from your job.

- **Protecting Emotional Integrity:** Boundaries protect your emotional well-being from undue stress, projection, or emotional labor imposed by others. They ensure that you do not take on the responsibility for other people's emotional states or poor choices, which is a major source of internal stress.
- **Defining Your Value:** When you set clear limits, you demonstrate that your time, energy, and needs are important. This action reinforces your internal self-respect and confirms to others that your needs must be considered in the social exchange, which, paradoxically, earns their respect.

Boundaries fall into several key categories: emotional (protecting your well-being), physical (defining your space), material (protecting belongings), time (protecting your schedule), and workplace (protecting work-life balance). Mastering the communication of these boundaries is the central focus of this book.

The Final Step: Integrity as the Highest Respect

The ability to set and maintain boundaries is ultimately rooted in **self-respect** and **integrity**.

Integrity means that your external behavior aligns with your core internal values, the principles that truly guide your decisions and actions. When you are forced to violate your boundaries, such as saying "yes" when you desperately want to say "no", you experience misalignment. This misalignment leads to stress, resentment, and a collapse in self-respect because your actions betrayed your inner sense of what is right.

The path forward requires deep self-reflection to clarify those guiding values: What aspects of your personality are you most proud of? When do you feel most in control of your life? This emotional self-reflection is itself supported by meta-analytic evidence for addressing negative emotional states like anxiety and depression.

By aligning your actions with your values, you establish consistency. An individual who is consistent, assertive, and respectful of their own needs is an individual who is predictable and trustworthy. This integrity is the highest form of respect you can offer yourself and others.

The 5-Part Action Plan for Defining Your Space

This final book synthesizes all the skills you have learned, calm, assertiveness, and self-worth, into a concrete, five-part plan for external integrity.

1. **Define the Limits (Chapter 2):** You will move from vague discomfort to establishing clear, structured boundaries across emotional, time, and workplace categories, treating them as non-negotiable requirements for mental health maintenance.

2. **Communicate with Conviction (Chapter 3):** You will use the assertive communication skills (DESC Script) and needs-based language (NVC) to voice your boundaries clearly, ensuring they are understood as declarations of self-care, not impositions of control.

3. **Audit the Exchange (Chapter 4):** You will learn how to systematically audit your key relationships using SET principles, ensuring fairness and reciprocity are maintained, and identifying where you need to assertively re-balance the rewards and costs.

4. **Validate Others (Chapter 5):** Spreading respect requires a move beyond self-focus. You will learn to give credit where due, actively validating the contributions and efforts of others, which reinforces prosocial motivation (Book 4) and counters hostile self-centeredness.

5. **Achieve Alignment (Chapter 6):** You will engage in deep self-reflection to clarify your core values and assess the current misalignment in your life. The goal is to make small, consistent behavioral choices that reflect your true self, cementing the highest form of self-respect.

The journey ends here, but the work of maintenance begins. You have the internal capacity. Now, you will learn the external skills to define your worth and maintain your peace forever.

CHAPTER 1

SET CLEAR LIMITS: ESTABLISHING BOUNDARIES FOR MENTAL HEALTH

You have internalized the necessity of respect as reciprocity. You know that if your relationships are to thrive, the rewards must balance the costs, and you must establish yourself as a high-value partner in that exchange.

The transition from intellectual understanding to practical execution begins here. This chapter is your instruction manual for the single, most necessary action required to maintain that balance: **setting boundaries**.

Many people view boundaries as inherently hostile, rigid demands that restrict freedom. This is entirely wrong. Boundaries are not tools for controlling other people. They are essential acts of self-care and declarations of self-respect. They are the limits you identify for yourself and apply through clear communication to maintain your security, health, and emotional stability in all relationships, at work and at home. If you fail to set limits, you guarantee that all the emotional and physiological resources you built in Books 1, 2, and 4 will be systematically drained until you are depleted and resentful.

Boundaries as a Non-Negotiable Act of Self-Care

Setting healthy boundaries is not a luxury. It is a critical component of maintaining your mental and emotional health. If you are struggling with chronic exhaustion, perpetual resentment, or a feeling that your life is not your own, it is a clear signal that your boundaries are weak or nonexistent.

The benefits of setting and maintaining clear boundaries are measurable and directly counteract the negative habits you are working to eliminate:

1. **Protecting Against Burnout:** Establishing clear boundaries, especially in professional environments (workplace boundaries), is a proven form of self-care that actively reduces the risk of **workplace burnout**. Burnout is a serious condition defined by chronic energy depletion, increased mental distance from one's job, and feelings of negativism related to work. When you fail to draw lines around your time and effort, you invite this depletion.

2. **Reinforcing Self-Respect:** When you set clear limits, you send an undeniable message to yourself and to the world: "My time, energy, and needs are important and worthy of protection." This action reinforces your internal sense of self-respect and integrity (Book 5, Chapter 6).

3. **Preventing Resentment:** Passive behavior, saying "yes" when you desperately mean "no", does not eliminate conflict. It merely delays it, turning it inward where it ferments as **resentment**. Resentment is repressed anger, which fuels irritability and eventual aggressive outbursts (reactive aggression, Book 2). Boundaries are the healthy emotional release valve that prevents this toxic buildup.

By defining your space, you are actively choosing to protect the emotional stability (low HRV, high gratitude) you built over the previous four books.

Identifying Your Boundary Categories

Boundaries are often complex because they apply to many different aspects of your life. Moving from vague discomfort to clear action requires identifying the specific category where your limits are being violated most frequently.

Boundaries fall into several key categories:

Boundary Type	Definition and Function	Example of a Clear Limit
Emotional Boundaries	Protecting your well-being from undue stress, projection, or emotional labor imposed by others. You are not responsible for managing another person's feelings.	"I can listen for five minutes, but I cannot be your crisis counselor; I need you to find professional help for that."
Time Boundaries	Protecting the use and misuse of your time, ensuring your schedule is respected and that commitments are honored.	"I do not check or respond to work emails after 5:30 PM, regardless of urgency."
Workplace Boundaries	Protecting your professional balance. This defines when and how you engage with professional duties outside of your designated time / role.	"I will communicate my working hours clearly in my email signature."
Physical Boundaries	Defining your physical space and comfort levels, including personal touch and proximity.	"I am not comfortable hugging people I have just met."
Material Boundaries	Protecting your personal belongings, money, or resources from being misused or taken without consent.	"Please ask before borrowing my tools, and please return them by the end of the day."

The first actionable step is auditing your life to find the category where you are experiencing the most frequent pain, stress, or resentment. That is the area that requires immediate attention and the implementation of a firm, well-communicated limit.

Action Tool 1: The Discomfort Audit

Most people recognize a boundary violation only *after* the fact, when they are already feeling anger or resentment. To set effective boundaries, you must learn to recognize the **early physical and emotional signals** that a limit is being crossed. This uses the self-reflection skills you mastered in Book 2 (recognizing early warning signs of anger/stress).

Action Focus: Connecting Signal to Source

Commit to auditing your emotional and physical responses over the next three days, looking for the physical manifestation of discomfort.

Signal (Internal Feeling / Sensation)	Source (External Action / Person)	Underlying Need Violated
Tightness in chest, anxiety surge (Book 2)	When my relative asks for financial help again.	**Autonomy, Financial Safety**
Immediate mental exhaustion, energy depletion (Burnout sign)	When my coworker dumps her weekend crisis on me every Monday morning.	**Emotional Boundary, Ease, Time**
Ruminating resentment (Chapter 3, Book 2)	When my spouse consistently leaves their work items on the shared kitchen table.	**Order, Respect for Shared Space**
Impulse to avoid or lie (Passive behavior)	When my manager asks me to take on a project outside of my scope after hours.	**Time Boundary, Professional Integrity**

By identifying the specific action that triggers the physical and emotional discomfort, you transition from saying "I feel bad" to stating the problem factually: "My time boundary is being crossed by requests after 5:30 PM." This clarity is essential, as it allows you to move to the next stage: establishing the limit.

Action Tool 2: Establishing Clarity—The "When/I will" Rule

A boundary is only effective if it is clear, specific, and backed by a predictable action on your part. Vague limits are easily crossed and quickly lead back to resentment.

The most effective boundaries follow the **"When X happens, I will do Y"** structure. This removes emotional volatility and frames the boundary as a statement of your personal action, not a demand for the other person's obedience.

1. Define the Limit Factually:

The limit must target a specific, observable behavior (Observation, NVC).

- *Ineffective Limit:* "Don't be so negative around me." (Too vague, easily denied.)
- *Factual Limit:* "When you start complaining about work for more than three minutes, or use judgmental language about our team."

2. Define Your Predictable Action:

The action must be something *you* control. This maintains your agency and integrity.

- *Ineffective Action:* "You need to change the subject." (Demands they change.)
- *Predictable Action:* "I will change the subject, or I will end the conversation and leave the room."

Example Boundary Scripts (Internal):

- **Time Boundary:** "When a meeting runs 10 minutes past the scheduled end time, **I will politely stand up and say I have a hard stop.**"

- **Emotional Boundary:** "When a friend starts calling me to exclusively complain about their partner for the third time this week, **I will interrupt and suggest they seek professional counseling.**"

- **Work Boundary:** "When a colleague emails me with a non-urgent request on Saturday, **I will not open the email and I will reply on Monday morning during scheduled hours.**"

This structured approach transforms the boundary from a subjective feeling into an objective rule, making it easier to enforce and harder for others to violate. You are utilizing the assertive communication skills (DESC script, Book 3) to deliver a clear, specific request (S: Specify) followed by a predictable consequence (C: Consequences), all framed around your core need for health and integrity.

Protecting Against Boundary Violation (The Backlash)

When you first begin setting boundaries, you will likely face resistance, resentment, or even anger from those accustomed to your passive compliance. This backlash is not proof that the boundary is wrong. It is proof that the old, inequitable system (SET) is being successfully disrupted.

To navigate this resistance, you must be prepared to protect the boundary with the emotional regulation you have mastered:

1. **Maintain Calm (Book 2):** When the other person becomes angry or aggressive, immediately revert to your physiological tools (4-7-8 breathing) to keep your PFC online. Their anger is a predictable cost of the relational exchange; do not let it trigger your reactive aggression.

2. **Repeat, Do Not Debate:** Avoid arguing, justifying, or over-explaining. You are not asking for permission; you are stating a fact about yourself. Repeat the boundary statement clearly and calmly. *Example: "I understand you are frustrated, but I still need to leave at 5:30 PM."*

3. **Follow Through:** This is the most crucial step. A boundary is not a verbal agreement; it is an action. If you state the limit, you must follow through with the consequence (e.g., leaving the room, not replying to the email) to prove to yourself and the other person that you mean it.

This consistent, predictable follow-through is what cements your self-respect and earns the respect of others. By moving away from vague discomfort to clear, consistent limits, you define your value and protect the internal peace you worked so hard to build.

CHAPTER 2

USE THE BOUNDARY SCRIPT: COMMUNICATING NEEDS WITH CONVICTION

You have completed the essential pre-work. You know that a boundary is a necessary act of self-care (Chapter 2), and you have successfully identified the specific areas where your time, energy, or emotional space are being violated. You have named the threat.

Now comes the hard part: the external execution.

A boundary is just a thought until it is voiced. The moment you move from internal decision to external communication, you face the fear of confrontation, rejection, or causing offense. This fear often leads people to deliver boundaries passively, with a whisper, a joke, or an apology, or aggressively, with a hostile demand that triggers immediate resistance. Both approaches destroy the boundary before it can take root.

The integrity of your internal peace depends on your ability to voice your limits with **conviction and care**. You need a precise, structural framework that guarantees your message is delivered clearly, reduces the listener's defensiveness, and aligns your external actions with your internal self-respect. This chapter gives you that framework by adapting your assertive communication skills (Book 3) to the high-stakes task of boundary setting.

The Anatomy of Conviction: Assertiveness as Integrity

A boundary is an assertive declaration. **Assertiveness** is the core skill that allows you to express your thoughts, feelings, and beliefs directly and honestly while strictly respecting the rights of others. When it comes to boundaries, assertiveness is not optional; it is the delivery system for mutual respect.

Why is assertive delivery necessary for a boundary to work?

1. **Passive Delivery Fails Integrity:** If you deliver a boundary passively, for example, saying, "I guess I really shouldn't work late again, maybe?", you send the message that the limit is negotiable. You signal that your needs are less important than the other person's potential discomfort. This fuels resentment in you (repressed anger) and teaches the other person that they can safely ignore your limit, driving the relational ledger back into inequity (Social Exchange Theory, Chapter 1).

2. **Aggressive Delivery Fails Connection:** If you deliver the boundary aggressively, for example, yelling, "Stop calling me after 6 PM! You are so selfish!", you trigger the listener's defense mechanisms. Their amygdala lights up, the PFC shuts down, and they stop hearing your need. The boundary gets lost in the static of their emotional reaction. Aggression may force temporary compliance through fear, but it destroys mutual trust, which is the long-term cost you are trying to avoid.

Assertive communication, when defining a boundary, is the middle path. It uses clear, direct language that avoids hostility, ensuring the message is about the *limit* and *your need*, not a judgment of the *other person's character*. This is why you built the internal calm in Book 2: to keep your physiology regulated while you execute this high-stakes script.

The Core Tool: The Boundary Script (DESC Adaptation)

You will use the **DESC Script** (Describe, Express, Specify, Consequences) as your primary tool for asserting boundaries. This structure forces clarity, prevents emotional tangents, and ensures you state both the limit and the non-hostile outcome.

When adapting the DESC script for a boundary, the focus shifts to defining your personal action rule.

D: Describe the Factual Violation

Start by describing the factual behavior that is violating your limit. This must be an objective **Observation** (NVC principle) that is verifiable and devoid of judgment or emotional language.

- **Action Rule:** Use neutral language to state the *specific*, recurring behavior that is the problem.
- *Ineffective:* "You are always dumping your problems on me."
- *Effective:* "I have noticed that for the last three weekends, you have called me on Sunday morning to discuss your work stress for over forty-five minutes."

E: Express the Impact on Your Needs

Next, you must connect the factual violation to the internal cost it is creating. This is where you use the vulnerability of "I" statements to express the resulting feeling and, crucially, the underlying **Need** (NVC principle) that is being violated.

- **Action Rule:** Connect the behavior to a genuine human need (e.g., rest, autonomy, safety, energy).
- *Ineffective:* "I feel like you don't respect me." (This is a blame word/judgment.)
- *Effective:* "I feel completely drained and overwhelmed by these lengthy calls. My deep need for **rest** and **emotional autonomy** on my one day off is not being met."

By defining the boundary in terms of your need for *rest*, you elevate the discussion from a petty demand to a necessary requirement for self-care.

S: Specify the New Action Rule (The Boundary)

This is the non-negotiable step. You must specify the clear, actionable rule you are setting moving forward. The limit must be clear, specific, and easily understood by the other person. This is your declaration of self-respect.

- **Action Rule:** State the limit directly, using a phrase that signals personal control.
- *Ineffective:* "I need you to stop being so dependent on me." (Vague, demands they change.)
- *Effective:* "I need to establish a time boundary: From now on, I can listen for a maximum of **fifteen minutes** on Sunday, and I need to hear you actively transition to a different topic."

C: Consequences (Specify Your Predictable Action)

The final step is to specify the consequence. Critically, this consequence must focus on the **predictable action that *you* will take** to enforce the boundary, not on punishing the other person. This maintains your agency and integrity.

- **Action Rule:** State the consequence calmly. It is a factual statement of what happens next if the limit is breached.
- *Ineffective:* "If you call me again, I will hang up, and I won't talk to you for a week." (Punishment/Aggression.)
- *Effective:* "If the call goes over fifteen minutes, I will calmly remind you of my time boundary and then **end the call**. I will not be able to answer your call again until Monday morning."

Case Study: Asserting a Workplace Boundary

The DESC script is particularly potent in the workplace, where boundaries often blur between professional hours and personal time (Workplace Boundaries, Chapter 2).

Scenario: Your manager frequently sends non-urgent tasks via text message after 8:00 PM, violating your time boundary and causing you anxiety.

DESC Step	Assertive Boundary Script	Purpose / Alignment
D: Describe	"I've noticed that I often receive task requests via text message from you after 8:00 PM and on weekends."	Factual **Observation** (Chapter 2, Book 3). Neutralizes defensiveness.
E: Express	"Receiving these messages late causes me to feel anxious and interrupt my family time, violating my need for **rest** and a clear **work-life balance**."	Links action to core **Need** (NVC) and internal cost (stress, burnout).
S: Specify	"I need us to establish that all non-emergency communications will be sent via email during standard business hours (9 AM–5 PM)."	Clear, **Specific** rule. Actionable requirement.

DESC Step	Assertive Boundary Script	Purpose / Alignment
C: **Consequences**	"If a non-emergency text is sent after hours, I will not open it or see it until the next morning at 9:00 AM. This way, I can ensure my focus and energy are maintained for peak productivity during the day."	States **My Action** (I will not open it) and frames the outcome as a **Positive Consequence** for the shared goal (productivity).

This script transforms the situation from a complaint about rudeness to a proposal for functional efficiency, which is a key reward in the workplace social exchange (SET).

The Neurocognitive Power of Assertion

Executing a boundary script successfully is a high-leverage action that reinforces every positive neural pathway you have built.

1. **Restoring Agency (Countering Helplessness):** Successfully asserting a boundary provides a massive, immediate psychological reward. You took purposeful action (Chapter 5, Book 1) and that action produced a result (the boundary was stated, your needs were defended). This measurable success triggers dopamine release, affirming your belief in personal agency and directly counteracting the neurochemical deficits of learned helplessness.

2. **Strengthening Self-Esteem and Coping:** Assertiveness itself is a core coping skill. By directly and respectfully standing up for your interests, you eliminate the toxic buildup of resentment (repressed anger). Research confirms that assertive communication helps control stress and anger, improves coping skills, boosts self-esteem, and earns the respect of others. The consistent practice of this skill reinforces your internal worth.

3. **Measurable Efficacy:** This is not anecdotal. Assertiveness training produces measurable behavioral change. Studies show that participants who undergo assertiveness training experience significant improvement in their assertiveness levels. For example, in clinical settings, 23.5% of participants improved their assertiveness category after structured training, compared to only 4% who regressed. Your structured script is the methodology for this measurable growth.

A boundary is not a verbal agreement; it is an action. The conviction behind the boundary rests entirely on your willingness to execute the stated consequence calmly and predictably.

When you first assert a boundary, you will inevitably face **backlash**. The other person is invested in the old, inequitable system where your compliance was the predictable reward. Their resistance, anger, guilt-tripping, or dismissal, is not proof that your boundary is wrong; it is proof that the old system is being successfully disrupted.

Navigating the Backlash:

1. **Emotional Regulation is Primary (Book 2):** Their anger will likely trigger your emotional warning signs. Immediately revert to your physiological tools (4-7-8 breathing) to keep your PFC online. Do not let their hostility trigger your reactive aggression.

2. **Repeat, Do Not Debate:** Do not fall into the trap of arguing or justifying the boundary. Your boundary is a statement of fact about your self-care, not an argument to be won. Calmly repeat the core limit: "I understand you are frustrated, but I still need to end the call now."

3. **Execute the Consequence:** If the limit is crossed, you must follow through with your stated action (C: Consequences). If you said you would end the call, you must end the call. This is the moment your integrity is tested. Consistent follow-through is what moves the boundary from a suggestion to a rule, cementing your self-respect and earning predictable respect from others.

By committing to the conviction of your script and the integrity of your follow-through, you define your value and protect the internal peace you worked so hard to build. This establishes the necessary stability to ensure fairness and reciprocity in all your most important relationships.

CHAPTER 3
HONOR THE EXCHANGE:
ENSURING FAIRNESS IN SOCIAL RELATIONSHIPS

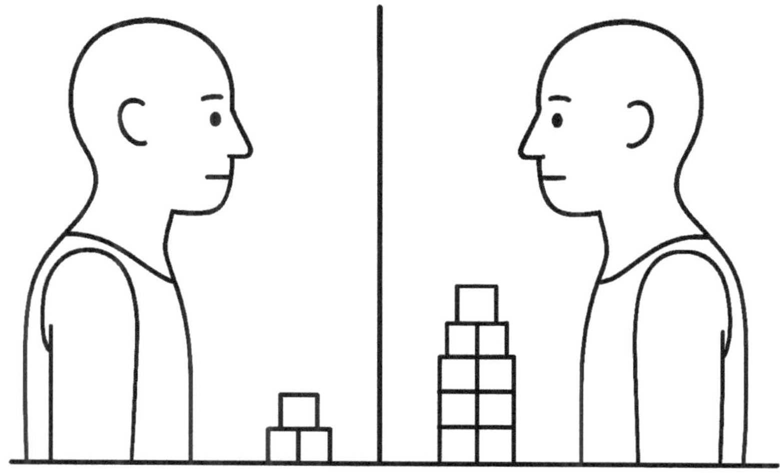

You have achieved the capacity for self-respect. You know how to set clear limits and communicate your boundaries assertively, using your calm voice to define your space (Chapter 3). This mastery is crucial because it ensures that your internal resources are protected from passive depletion.

But boundaries are only half of the equation. To truly **spread respect**, you must actively audit the health of your most important relationships. Respect is not a feeling; it is a calculation of fairness, and it is governed by the principles of **reciprocity**.

This chapter provides the tools for that audit. We will use the framework of **Social Exchange Theory (SET)** to identify where your relationships are imbalanced, where you are allowing costs to accumulate, and where you need to assertively negotiate a more equitable contribution. Healthy relationships are built on balanced exchanges, not martyrdom or constant, unreciprocated effort.

The Scientific Principle: The Norm of Reciprocity

Social Exchange Theory (SET) is the foundational concept for understanding how respect functions in relationships. As established in the introduction, SET states that social behavior results from weighing the **rewards** received against the **costs** incurred.

The stability of all social relationships, from professional partnerships to family dynamics, depends heavily on the **norm of reciprocity**. This social contract suggests two things:

1. **Return Benefits:** People should return the benefits or rewards they receive from others.

2. **Avoid Unreciprocated Obligation:** People try to avoid creating or sustaining relationships where they are consistently giving more than they receive, or vice versa.

In the relational ledger, emotional energy, time, support, and financial resources are all viewed as *costs* or *investments*. Kindness, respect, and validation are *rewards*. A relationship is deemed successful and stable when the rewards and costs for both parties are perceived as roughly balanced, or **equitable**.

If you consistently give more emotional energy, time, or support than you receive, if your costs always outweigh your rewards, the exchange will be viewed as inequitable, and the relationship will eventually become unstable, often leading to resentment and breakdown.

The Problem of Inequity: Comparison Levels

The feeling that a relationship is unfair is not just based on the absolute rewards you receive. It is based on a psychological benchmark called the **comparison level (CL)**.

Your comparison level is your personal standard. It is what you believe you deserve to receive in a specific type of relationship, based on past experience and social context.

- **Relationship A (CL Violation):** If you are consistently listening to a friend's problems for two hours a week, but they cancel every time you need support, you are violating your comparison level for a *reciprocal friendship*. Your costs are high; your rewards are low.

- **The Internal Cost:** This violation damages your self-respect and fuels the toxic buildup of resentment (repressed anger, Book 2, Chapter 3). You feel exploited, undervalued, and angry, even if you never express it.

Identifying inequity is crucial for both self-respect and relational longevity. You must stop allowing inequitable exchanges to deplete your resources and violate your standard of worth.

Action Tool 1: The Relational Ledger Audit

You must transition from vague feelings of being "used" to objective identification of inequity. The Relational Ledger Audit forces you to quantify the exchange in your key relationships using the SET framework.

Action Focus: Auditing Investments and Returns

Choose three key relationships (one professional, one personal, one family) where you feel chronic stress or resentment. Audit the exchange over the last month by focusing only on observable actions.

Relationship Partner	My Investment (Costs / Effort)	Their Contribution (Rewards / Return)	Equity Status (Balanced / Deficit)
Colleague (Jerry)	Spent 3 hours fixing Jerry's error; offered validation after his review.	Jerry gave one five-minute compliment; failed to attend my presentation.	**Deficit.** My emotional and time cost significantly outweighs the return.
Friend (Sarah)	Listened to her job stress for 4 phone calls; initiated all plans.	Sarah sent a thoughtful birthday card; listened intently to my one problem.	**Slight Deficit.** Rewards are high quality, but I carry all the labor of initiation.

The Principle: If you consistently identify a **Deficit** in the relationship, you have discovered a boundary problem that needs assertive communication. The current exchange is violating your comparison level, and it is a drain on your emotional resources (your inner strength). This relationship is a liability to your sustained peace.

Action Tool 2: Negotiating Reciprocity with Assertiveness

Once you identify an inequity, you cannot wait for the other person to change magically. You must assertively communicate the need for a more equitable contribution. This is the moment where your Kind Speech skills (Book 3) become the tools for self-defense.

Action Focus: Using DESC to Rebalance the Ledger

You must use the **DESC Script** (Describe, Express, Specify, Consequences) to initiate the conversation, focusing on the need for fairness (equity).

Scenario: You audited your relationship with your colleague, Jerry, and identified a consistent deficit of effort and support.

DESC Step	Script for Asserting Reciprocity	Principle
D: Describe	"Jerry, I noticed that I spent about three hours fixing that bug in your code last week, and I spent an hour listening to your concerns about your review, but you missed my presentation yesterday."	Neutral **Observation** (Facts).
E: Express	"I felt depleted and unsupported by that exchange. I need our working relationship to meet my need for **equity** and **mutual support**."	Links feeling to core **Need** (NVC).
S: Specify	"I need us to agree on a better balance. For our relationship to continue working well, I need you to be present and engaged during my major professional events."	**Specific** request for observable behavior (Attendance / Engagement).
C: Consequences	"If we both commit to being present and engaged for each other's key moments, we both benefit from higher visibility and confidence. If I cannot rely on this, I will need to limit my assistance to only urgent, immediate tasks."	States the **Positive Consequence** (mutual benefit) and your predictable **Action** (re-setting the boundary / limit) if the inequity persists.

This assertive action reinforces mutual respect and prevents you from feeling exploited or depleted. You are not fighting; you are simply maintaining the health of the social contract.

The Role of Integrity in the Exchange

The ability to successfully negotiate reciprocity is deeply linked to your internal integrity (Book 5, Chapter 6).

If you value **kindness** (Book 4), you must be willing to give support. But if you also value **self-respect** and **autonomy**, you must be willing to defend your limits. When you assertively demand equity, you are aligning your actions with your values: you respect the other person enough to be honest (kindness), and you respect yourself enough to be firm (autonomy).

When you follow through on the consequence (C: Consequences), you prove that your boundary is not arbitrary, it is rooted in a non-negotiable value. This consistent follow-through is what moves the boundary from a mere suggestion to a reliable relational fact, which in turn earns the respect and trust of others.

Respect as a Living Agreement

Respect is not a given; it is a living agreement that requires continuous auditing and negotiation. By using the principles of Social Exchange Theory, you gain the objective, rational framework needed to identify and correct inequity.

You now possess the tools to ensure that your relationships are balanced, fair, and mutually rewarding. You have moved from passively enduring unbalanced relationships to actively and competently creating healthy, reciprocal exchanges. This foundation of fairness ensures that your inner strength is protected and that the integrity of your actions is always aligned with your highest self-respect.

CHAPTER 4

GIVE CREDIT WHERE DUE: RESPECTING OTHERS' CONTRIBUTIONS AND AGENCY

You've come this far because you stood up for yourself. You've learned to set firm boundaries, express your true needs, and check whether your relationships are fair and balanced (Chapter 4). This strong focus on valuing yourself is important. It helps protect your emotional energy.

But respect isn't something you can just keep to yourself like a treasure. It's more like a flowing exchange where both sides give and take. If you only pay attention to what you deserve, you might slip into a different kind of self-focus. You might start noticing only your own hard work and forget to appreciate what others bring to the table.

Here's the simple truth: One big problem with old, unhealthy habits is not recognizing the effort, sacrifices, and worth of the people you depend on. Ignoring this, failing to give credit where it's due, makes your new kindness seem hollow. It can look like you care only about your side of things.

This chapter talks about the last key step in respect: really recognizing others' efforts and choices. This skill makes sure your clear words come with true appreciation behind them. Giving credit isn't just polite, it's a crucial way to build strong social bonds, boost your own happiness, and push back against the selfishness and hostility of old habits.

The Cost of Staying Quiet: Minimizing Others' Work

If you think back to times you were rude or dismissive, it's often because you lost perspective. You were stuck on your own pain and effort, and couldn't see what the other person was doing or intending.

This failure to recognize others often comes from harmful mental patterns:

- Minimizing and Mislabeling: This is when you downplay someone else's effort or intentions. For example, when a coworker finishes a task, your mind might say, "That was easy for them," or "They were just doing their job." This stops you from seeing their work as a real contribution in your relationship. When you don't give back, it quickly leads to imbalance and resentment. Studies show that hostile behavior can often be linked to these types of mental errors where people undervalue others to feel better about themselves.

- The Blame Habit: Just like anger can lead to blaming others, rude behavior often comes with refusing to own up to shared problems while pointing fingers at others. Focusing only on someone's flaws stops you from noticing their good work. This lack of credit harms relationships. It denies people the basic need to be seen and appreciated and weakens the motivation to keep investing effort. When people's efforts are always ignored, staying involved feels too costly.

Why Recognition Matters: A Helpful Action

Giving credit and recognizing others is a strong, intentional way to be helpful, it shows you care about their feelings and rights. This kindness is the outward sign of the gratitude you've built inside (Book 4).

Benefits of Giving Recognition:

- Lifts Your Mood: When you genuinely recognize someone else, you get a mood boost in return. It's the brain's reward for being kind. Studies show people who regularly help others feel happier and experience fewer bad moods. Being generous in this way helps keep your own emotional balance strong.

- Reduces Stress: Helping others by recognizing their effort shifts your focus away from your own worries, lowering your stress levels. This mental shift works well with the calming strategies you learned earlier (Book 2).

- Strengthens Give and Take: Giving credit is a simple, low-effort way to add value to your relationships. When you acknowledge a coworker's role, they feel appreciated and are encouraged to keep cooperating. This makes your connections steadier and more positive (Find-Remind-Bind Theory, Book 4).

So, giving recognition isn't just about making others feel good, it's also key to your own mental health and to building strong, lasting relationships.

Action Tool 1: Recognize Effort and Intent

The main goal here is to make sure the other person feels truly "seen" for the work they put in, not just for the final result. Be clear and specific about what you notice, focusing on how they did it more than just what they achieved.

Action Steps:

- Try to give three specific compliments today, pointing out effort and the process.

- Focus on effort, not just results. Instead of saying, "Your presentation was great," say, "I noticed how much you practiced for that presentation; your preparation really showed."

- Focus on intent, not just outcome. Instead of "The house looks clean," try, "I appreciate how you cleaned the kitchen to give me a break; that really means a lot."

- Recognize effort even when things don't turn out perfectly. For example, "That solution didn't work, but I really value the initiative you took to research it. We'll use what you learned next time."

Doing this kind of focused recognition makes your praise feel real and valuable, encouraging others to keep being helpful toward you.

Action Tool 2: The Power of Public Credit

In groups, whether at work, with friends, or family, giving credit publicly is a great way to spread respect and build positivity. When others see recognition being shared openly, it sends a strong message of generosity.

Action Steps:

- When you get praise for a team's success, quickly give credit to others who helped. For example, say, "Thanks, but this success really comes down to Sarah's careful data work and David's patience with the client."
- Even in simple talks, recognize someone's role in supporting a point. For example, "That's a good point, and I appreciate you speaking up to make it clear for everyone."

This shows you have enough confidence in yourself not to hoard credit. Sharing recognition like this builds trust and marks you as a supportive leader and teammate.

Respect Flows Both Ways

By mastering how to show respect outwardly, you complete a big transformation. You've set your limits to protect your peace. You've checked for fairness in your dealings. Now you add the step of giving credit and recognition to others.

Doing this consistently makes your relationships healthier and more balanced. When you show appreciation, it encourages others to keep giving their best, stabilizing your social circle (Find-Remind-Bind Theory).

You've shifted from hostile habits to generous actions. You give respect and expect it back. This flow keeps your inner strength safe and your outer life honest. The final chapter will help you tie this all together by living out your core values.

CHAPTER 5

LIVE YOUR VALUES:

ALIGNING BEHAVIOR WITH SELF-RESPECT

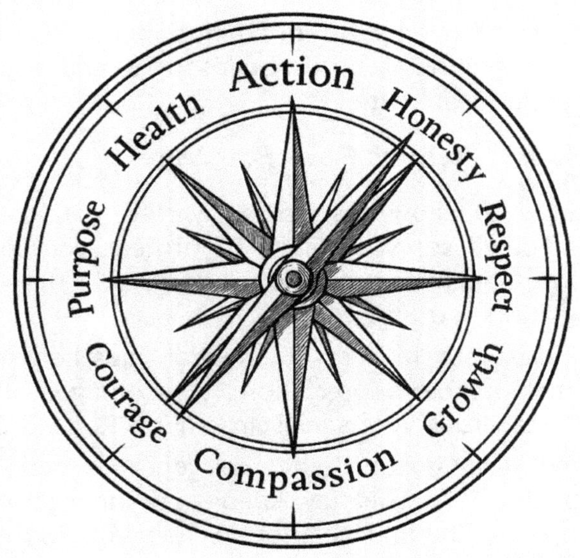

You have reached the final layer of self-respect. You have built the external defense system: clear boundaries, assertive scripts, and a commitment to reciprocal fairness (Chapters 2–5). This structural work ensures that your relationships are balanced and protected from exploitation.

But all these external actions are fragile if they are not rooted in an internal anchor. If you stand up for your time (a time boundary) but deep down you don't believe your work is meaningful, the boundary will eventually collapse. If you apologize for hostile speech (relational repair) but your actions immediately fall back into old, selfish patterns, your words lack authenticity.

The ultimate measure of respect, and the final action required for permanent change, is **integrity**. Integrity means that your external behavior aligns perfectly with your core internal values, the principles that truly guide your decisions and actions. When your actions betray your values, you experience immediate, measurable distress. This chapter teaches you how to identify those core values and systematically align your daily choices with them, cementing the highest form of self-respect.

The Problem of Misalignment: When Actions Betray Beliefs

Everyone holds a set of core values, deep-seated beliefs about what is good, right, and worthwhile (e.g., honesty, freedom, connection, competence, health). These values are the blueprint for your ideal self.

However, the destructive habits of negativity and hostility create a profound state of **misalignment** between that ideal blueprint and your daily reality.

- **The Cost of Betrayal:** Misalignment occurs when you consistently choose an action that contradicts a core value. For example, if your core value is **Honesty**, but you routinely tell small lies or omit facts to avoid difficult conversations, you are betraying yourself. If your core value is **Health**, but you chronically overwork and sacrifice sleep, you are violating your own integrity.

- **The Psychological Toll:** When behavior deviates substantially from clear values, the result is chronic stress, feelings of inauthenticity, and a severe collapse in self-respect. You feel out of control and disconnected from your true self. This emotional distress is a powerful trigger for reverting to old negative patterns, like passive-aggressive behavior or rumination (Book 2).

The commitment in this chapter is to close the gap between who you say you are and what you actually do. This consistency, this integrity, is what makes your asserted boundaries feel unshakable.

Action Tool 1: The Core Value Clarification Audit

You cannot align your life with values you cannot clearly name. The first step is deep, intentional self-reflection to clarify your true guiding principles. This self-reflection is supported by meta-analytic evidence as an effective tool for addressing negative emotional states like anxiety and depression.

Action Focus: Defining Your Personal Constitution

Ask yourself these four foundational questions. Write down one to three words that represent the core value that guides your answer.

1. **Identity:** What aspects of your personality are you most proud of, even when they are challenged? (This reveals values like **Courage** or **Kindness.**)
2. **Fulfillment:** When do you feel most fulfilled, capable, and authentically yourself? (This reveals values like **Competence** or **Connection.**)
3. **Control:** When do you feel most in control of your life, and what conditions created that feeling? (This reveals values like **Autonomy** or **Order.**)
4. **Aspiration:** If you knew you could not fail, what would your life look like? (This reveals values like **Impact** or **Contribution.**)

Your Result: Compile a list of your 5 to 7 highest-ranking values (e.g., Health, Honesty, Connection, Autonomy, Competence). This list becomes your personal constitution, the objective standard against which all future decisions are measured.

Action Tool 2: The Alignment Assessment

Once your values are clear, you must ruthlessly assess the current level of misalignment in your daily life. This is the moment where you apply the clear, factual observation skills of NVC (Book 3) to your own behavior.

Action Focus: Identifying the Integrity Gaps

Choose your top three core values. For each value, identify one specific habit or boundary failure that is actively undermining it.

Core Value	Specific Misaligned Habit	Cost of Misalignment
Health	Routinely accepting late-night calls, leading to less than 6 hours of sleep.	Violates the basic need for rest; weakens PFC and emotional regulation (Book 2).
Honesty	Telling "white lies" to a partner to avoid difficult conflict about finances.	Erodes trust (relational cost) and causes internal anxiety / shame (personal cost).
Autonomy	Saying "yes" to colleagues' last-minute requests when my schedule is already full.	Leads to resentment and violates the time boundary (Chapter 2); reinforces passive behavior.

The identification of these gaps is the most powerful step. It moves the feeling of being "stuck" from a vague emotional problem to a concrete, solvable behavioral problem. You realize: "My anxiety is not random; it is the natural consequence of betraying my value of Health through poor sleep."

Action Tool 3: Behavioral Alignment Through Small Wins

Closing the integrity gap requires committing to small, measurable behavioral choices that directly honor your values. This uses the principle of **Action to Create Hope** (Book 1, Chapter 5), affirming that your efforts produce results and rebuilding your sense of agency.

Action Focus: SMART Alignment Goals

For each misalignment identified, create a small, manageable, **SMART** goal that aligns your behavior with the value immediately.

Value and Gap	Actionable Alignment Goal (SMART)	Reinforcing Principle
Health (Less than 6 hours sleep)	**Goal:** Tonight, I will turn off all screens and be in bed by 10:30 PM, regardless of task completion.	Honors the **Time Boundary** (Chapter 2) and reinforces the value of Health.
Honesty (White lies about money)	**Goal:** This week, I will draft the DESC Script (Book 3) to initiate an honest, factual conversation about our spending limit on Thursday evening.	Uses **Assertive Communication** to align with Honesty; replaces avoidance with competence.
Autonomy (Saying yes when busy)	**Goal:** The next time a colleague makes a last-minute request, I will pause, check my calendar, and assertively say, "Thank you for asking; I will need to check my capacity and get back to you in an hour."	Uses **Behavioral Inhibition** (Book 2) to pause the passive impulse and honor the boundary.

This process ensures that every word you speak and every action you take is a deliberate choice that reflects your true self and your vision of success. This internal consistency is not only emotionally rewarding, it generates the highest form of self-respect.

The ability to live your values with consistency is the ultimate outcome of mastering respect. You have moved from a place where negative habits defined your character to a place where deliberate, value-driven actions define your integrity.

This integrity is the most powerful resource for maintaining the entire system:

- **Boundary Enforcement:** When you know a boundary is tied to your non-negotiable value of **Health** or **Autonomy**, it becomes infinitely easier to enforce it calmly and predictably (Chapter 3). You are not being mean; you are simply upholding your personal constitution.

- **Trust and Reciprocity:** People trust an individual whose actions are predictable and whose values are clear. This consistency is a high reward in the social exchange (SET, Chapter 4), stabilizing your relationships and earning you predictable respect.

You have defined your space. You have asserted your value. Now, you live the change. The final chapter summarizes the maintenance required to ensure a life of sustained integrity and mutual respect.

CONCLUSION
A LIFE OF INTEGRITY: SUSTAINING MUTUALLY RESPECTFUL INTERACTIONS

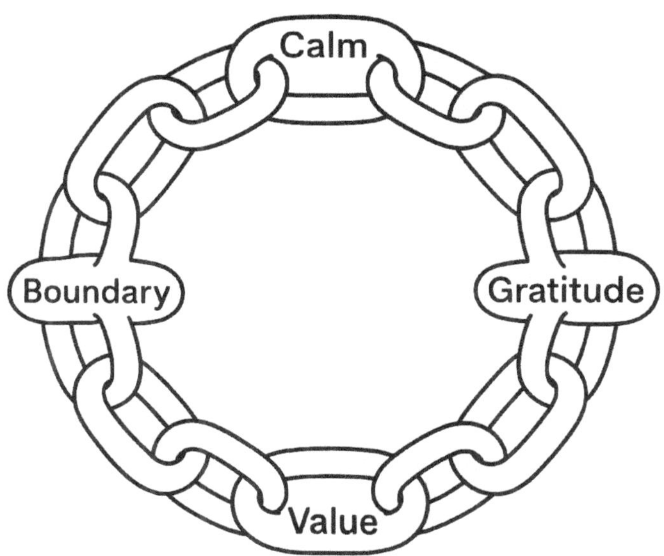

You have completed the entire process. This book was the final test. It moved you from internal self-worth to external action, ensuring that your life is defined by consistency, boundaries, and mutual respect.

The transformation across these five books is total. You replaced the chaotic cycles of negativity, rudeness, and hostility with a self-sustaining system of calm, clarity, and integrity. You did not just learn how to *feel* better; you learned how to *be* better, a predictable, reliable, and respectful agent in all your relationships.

This final chapter serves as a summation of the whole system, confirming how the external integrity you mastered here is the key to maintaining every single positive change you made. The life you want, one of deep connection and unwavering self-respect, depends on your commitment to this continuous maintenance.

The durable success of this program rests on the fact that every skill is interconnected. The skills you learned in the first four books are the resources you spend here in Book 5 to define and defend your value.

1. The Anchor: Integrity and Values

The ultimate foundation for sustained respect is **integrity**, the perfect alignment between your words, your actions, and your core values (Chapter 6).

- **The Action:** You identified your highest values (e.g., Health, Honesty, Autonomy) and audited your life for **misalignment** (Action Tool 2, Chapter 6). You committed to small, measurable **SMART** goals that directly honored those values (e.g., going to bed on time to honor Health).

- **The Result:** This consistency generates the highest form of self-respect. When you uphold your values, your boundaries (Chapter 2) become non-negotiable. You are not being mean when you say "no" to a late request; you are simply upholding your personal constitution. This conviction is what earns respect from others, stabilizing the relational exchange.

2. The Defense System: Boundaries and Assertiveness

Integrity makes your defense system predictable and effective, preventing the slow drain of resentment and burnout.

- **The Action:** You learned to set firm, specific **boundaries** (Chapter 2) and communicate them with conviction using the **DESC Script** (Chapter 3). This forces you to assert your needs clearly and respectfully, rather than falling into passive compliance or aggressive demands (Book 3).

- **The Result:** Assertive action directly reduces stress and prevents the toxic buildup of resentment (repressed anger, Book 2) that fuels future hostile outbursts. By taking control of your time, emotional energy, and professional space, you protect the emotional reserves you built through gratitude (Book 4). This protects against burnout, which is a major symptom of weak boundaries.

3. The Exchange: Reciprocity and Prosocial Flow

Your external interactions are now defined by fairness and generosity, replacing the old habits of minimization and self-centeredness.

- **The Action:** You mastered the **Relational Ledger Audit** (Chapter 4) to identify and assertively correct inequitable exchanges (SET). Simultaneously, you committed to actively **giving credit where due** (Chapter 5), acknowledging the effort and agency of others.

- **The Result:** This commitment to **reciprocity** ensures that your relationships are mutually beneficial, not exploitative. By reinforcing the goodness received (through validation), you motivate others to contribute goodness back, stabilizing the entire social system (Find-Remind-Bind Theory, Book 4). You are moving from a hostile, scarcity-based mindset to one of generous, sustainable abundance.

Maintenance: The Action Plan for Sustained Integrity

The transformation is complete, but the maintenance is continuous. Your daily practice must now integrate all five systems to ensure that the entire mechanism of control, clarity, and competence remains functional.

When a crisis occurs, when you feel the heat of anger, the urge to be rude, or the collapse of self-respect, you must use this integrated action sequence:

1. **Immediate Physiological Check (Book 2):** When you feel the first sign of stress or anger (the "burn"), immediately engage the **4-7-8 breathing protocol** to prevent cognitive shutdown. Calm the body first.

2. **Cognitive Audit (Book 1):** With your PFC back online, quickly check your interpretation: Are you using the **Hostile Attribution Bias** (Book 2) or **Catastrophizing** (Book 1)? Is the thought aligned with your core value of **Honesty** or **Fairness** (Book 5, Chapter 6)?

3. **Assertive Response (Book 3 & 5):** If a boundary has been crossed, or a need is unmet, do not ruminate (Book 2). Instead, immediately prepare and deliver the **DESC Boundary Script** (Chapter 3) or the **Accountable Apology** (Book 3, Chapter 6).

4. **Problem-Solving (Book 2):** Once calm and asserted, move immediately to the **5-Step Problem-Solving Model** to address the root cause of the conflict, ensuring a constructive solution replaces the impulsive reaction.

5. **Re-Focus and Recharge (Book 4):** Use the **Gratitude Journal** and the **HEAL Method** (Book 1) to restore your positive affect. By focusing on what remains and savoring a small moment of peace,

you lower cortisol and replenish the emotional reserves spent during the conflict.

This integrated system ensures that you respond to any threat not with the old default of negativity and hostility, but with deliberate, competent, and respectful action.

The Call to a Life of Integrity

You now possess the complete toolkit for defining your destiny. You have proven that every word, thought, and action is a choice you can control. You have moved from a place where you felt like a passive victim of your emotions to a place where you are the assertive, responsible agent of your life.

The ultimate reward is not just reduced stress, but genuine **integrity**, the unshakable self-respect that comes from knowing your external life perfectly reflects your highest internal values. This integrity is the foundation of a life where mutual respect is predictable, conflict is constructive, and kindness is effortless.

Live the change.

REFLECTION QUESTIONS

1. Identify one core personal value (e.g., Health, Honesty, Autonomy) that you violated this past week. Describe the specific misaligned habit and state the small, measurable **SMART goal** you will implement immediately to realign your behavior.

2. Describe one boundary you successfully asserted (or failed to assert) using the **DESC Script** this week. If you succeeded, what part of the script was most powerful? If you failed, what specific consequence did you fail to execute?

3. Audit one key relationship using the **Relational Ledger Audit** (Chapter 4). What specific, quantifiable investment (cost) are you putting in that is not being reciprocated, and what assertive request will you make to re-balance that exchange?

4. Describe one successful instance where you gave **Public Credit** or specific validation to someone (Chapter 5). How did this act of generosity reinforce your own sense of abundance (Book 4), and what was the immediate positive response from the recipient?

5. Reflecting on the entire five-book series: Identify one skill from Book 2 (Calm Anger) and one skill from Book 5 (Spread Respect) that you used together this week to achieve integrity. (e.g., Used 4-7-8 breathing to calmly enforce a Time Boundary).

OVERALL CONCLUSION

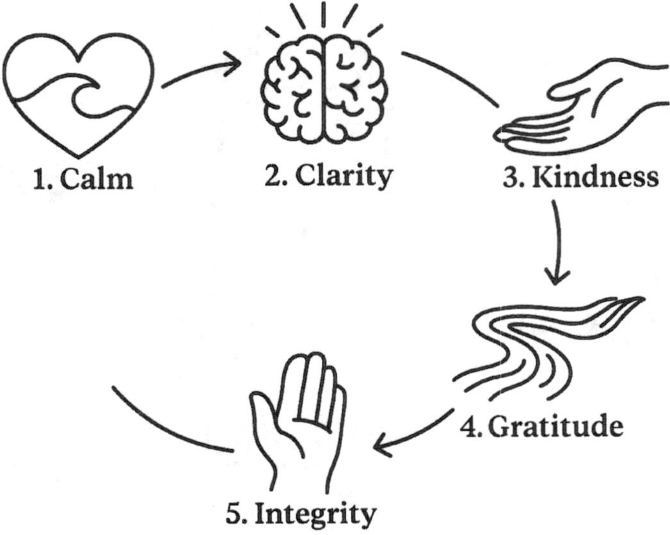

From Negative to Effective: Synthesizing the Five Skills

You have reached the end of the structural phase of this program. You replaced chronic, damaging habits with a complete, integrated system for living with integrity. You did not just learn coping tricks; you leveraged neuroplasticity to physically change the pathways in your brain that once dictated negativity, rudeness, and hostility.

The final strength of this transformation lies in the fact that your five books are not separate courses. They form a closed, self-sustaining system where each skill is the necessary prerequisite and resource for the next. This sequence ensures that your change is durable.

1. The Physiological Prerequisite: Calm Enables Clarity

The journey began by securing the body's state, recognizing that you cannot reason your way out of a physiological alarm.

- **Book 2 (Calm Anger)** provides the essential physical regulation: the **4-7-8 breathing protocol** and the control over your vagus nerve. This immediate intervention stops the adrenaline surge, lowers your heart rate, and prevents the emotional brain (amygdala) from hijacking your actions.

- **The Connection to Book 1 (Positivity):** This physical calm is the non-negotiable step that restores resources to your **Prefrontal Cortex (PFC)**. Without a regulated PFC, you cannot successfully execute the cognitive work of Book 1: identifying the **Triple Column Technique (TCT)** distortions or challenging your **Catastrophizing**. The calm body *enables* the rational mind.

2. The Internal Engine: Agency Fuels Generosity

Once the mind is calm and clear, you built the internal engine for action, ensuring motivation does not collapse when things get difficult.

- **Book 1 (Positivity)** and **Book 4 (Gratitude)** solved the problem of inertia. By committing to small, successful **SMART goals** (Book 1, Chapter 5), you directly counteracted **learned helplessness**, affirming agency and restoring the flow of dopamine necessary for motivation and hope.

- **The Connection to Resilience:** This internal engine is continuously maintained by **Gratitude (Book 4)**. Daily journaling and savoring lower your stress hormone, **cortisol**. This chemical stability acts as an emotional buffer, ensuring that when setbacks occur, you approach them from a position of abundance and resource (resilience), rather than deficit and panic.

3. The External System: Integrity Commands Respect

The stable, resourceful, and calm internal self must then define its space in the world.

- **Book 3 (Kind Speech)** provides the communication framework: the **Nonviolent Communication (NVC)** model and the **DESC Script**. These tools ensure that you articulate your needs and feelings clearly and respectfully, replacing the old, destructive language of blame and demands.

- **The Connection to Book 5 (Respect):** This assertive communication is the essential tool for **Book 5 (Respect)**. You use the DESC script to establish clear, non-negotiable **boundaries** (Chapter 3, Book 5). This action prevents the accumulation of costs (time, energy, resentment) that otherwise destroy the relational balance (Social Exchange Theory, Chapter 4, Book 5). When you speak assertively and honor your values, you stabilize your relationships and earn predictable respect.

The system is a loop: Calm body (Book 2) enables clear thought (Book 1), which fuels generous action (Book 4), which is then used to define and defend your space (Book 5), protecting the resources needed to remain calm (Book 2). Your commitment to integrity ensures this loop runs without interruption.

Action Maintenance: How to Troubleshoot Setbacks

The shift you have achieved is permanent, but maintenance is required. A resilient life is not one without problems. It is one where you have a predictable, structured sequence to follow when problems occur.

When you inevitably face an internal regression, a moment of rage, a slip into passive avoidance, or a wave of self-criticism, you must immediately treat the event not as a personal failure, but as a **system failure** that requires troubleshooting.

The 5-Phase Troubleshooting Sequence:

Phase 1: The Physiological Reset (Stop the Surge)

- **The Signal:** You feel the physical "burn": rapid heart rate, jaw clenching, shallow breath. You are experiencing sympathetic overdrive.

- **The Intervention:** Stop all external action. Immediately revert to the **4-7-8 breathing protocol**. Execute four full cycles (4-second inhale, 7-second hold, 8-second exhale). Your only job is to restore physiological calm.

- **The Test:** Re-check your heart rate or subjective tension. Did the physical symptoms measurably decrease? If not, repeat the breathing or use a physical redirect (walking, stretching) until calm is regained.

Phase 2: The Cognitive Diagnostic (Check the Story)

- **The Signal:** A torrent of angry, judgmental, or helpless thoughts floods your mind, often fueled by rumination.

- **The Intervention:** Engage the **Triple Column Technique (TCT)** (Book 1, Chapter 2). Identify the specific **Cognitive Distortion** (**Catastrophizing, Blaming Others, Labeling**). Ask the core question: **What is the objective, factual evidence for this thought?**

- **The Test:** Does the thought align with your core values (Book 5, Chapter 6)? If the thought contradicts **Honesty** or **Fairness**, dismiss it as an irrational pattern and immediately focus on a constructive thought replacement.

Phase 3: The Relational Correction (Reassert Integrity)

- **The Signal:** You realize you said "yes" when you meant "no," or you allowed a boundary to be violated, leading to resentment (SET inequity).

- **The Intervention:** Formulate and deliver a correction using the **DESC Assertive Script** (Book 3, Chapter 3 and Book 5, Chapter 3). You are not apologizing for the boundary; you are asserting your limit. Your delivery must be calm (due to Phase 1) and firm.

- **The Test:** Did you follow through on the consequence? If you fail to execute the consequence, the boundary collapses. Immediately schedule a specific time to re-assert the limit and execute the necessary consequence (e.g., cutting the meeting short, turning off the phone).

Phase 4: The Agency Restoration (Action to Overcome Inertia)

- **The Signal:** You feel overwhelmed, immobilized, or hopeless, the signature of **learned helplessness**.

- **The Intervention:** Choose the **smallest possible SMART goal** that honors a core value (Book 1, Chapter 5 and Book 5, Chapter 6). This is a guaranteed, low-cost win (e.g., spending 15 minutes organizing one drawer, sending one difficult email).

- **The Test:** Did you complete the specific action? Completion instantly triggers the dopamine reward, affirming your agency and breaking the cycle of inertia.

Phase 5: The Resilience Recharge (Refill the Well)

- **The Signal:** You feel emotionally depleted, experiencing low mood or increased irritability.

- **The Intervention:** Use the **HEAL Method** (Book 1) or engage in structured **Gratitude Journaling** (Book 4). Savor a small moment of competence or safety for 15 to 30 seconds, focusing on the physical sensation of contentment.

- **The Test:** Did you choose to focus on what **remains** (resources) rather than what is **lost** (deficits)? This continuous positive sensitization lowers stress chemistry and replenishes your emotional well-being.

You now possess the complete, scientific blueprint for a life defined by respect and clarity. This is no longer a self-help book; it is a reference manual for your new operating system.

The only remaining action is maintenance.

1. **Commit to Daily Check-ins:** Continue your daily Gratitude Journaling (Book 4) and your morning LKM/Mindfulness practice (Book 1). These habits are the low-cost investments that maintain high emotional returns (low stress, high resilience).

2. **Treat Boundaries as Sacred:** Your boundaries are the physical expression of your self-respect. Never violate them for the comfort of others. The moment you compromise your integrity, you invite hostility and negativity back into your life.

3. **Lead with Kindness and Accountability:** Use your skills to actively contribute to the social contract. Be assertive, not aggressive. Give credit where due. And when you inevitably fail, use the **Accountable Apology** (Book 3, Chapter 6) and the **Problem-Solving Model** (Book 2, Chapter 5) to repair the rift and strengthen the bond.

The transformation is yours. Go live a life of integrity, clarity, and unwavering self-respect.

CHECKLIST:

YOUR PRINT AND GO SHEET TO KEEP AND REVISIT

This sheet is your summary of the **Action Maintenance System**. It moves you from internal regulation to external integrity. Use this list daily and especially when you feel the first signs of stress, anger, or inertia.

System	Daily Action Plan: Maintenance & Prevention	Crisis Intervention: Stop the Surge
Book 4: Inner Strength (Recharge)	**Gratitude Savoring:** Write down 3 specific things you are grateful for. Focus on the *why* and *how*, savoring the feeling for 15 seconds.	**Resilience Check (Chapter 5):** When facing loss or anxiety, identify what **remains** (resources, health, network) rather than focusing on the deficit.
Book 1: Positivity (Cognitive Reset)	**HEAL Method:** Actively enrich and absorb one small positive moment for 15 seconds.	**TCT Audit (Chapter 2):** Immediately identify and label the core thought error (**Catastrophizing, Blaming Others, Labeling**).

Book 5: Respect (Integrity)	**Value Alignment:** Review your top 3 core values (Health, Honesty, etc.). Commit to one small **SMART action** today that honors one of these values.	**Relational Ledger Audit (Chapter 4):** Check the exchange. If resentment is present, define the specific **inequity** that needs asserting.
Book 5: Respect (Giving Credit)	**Prosocial Action:** Give one piece of specific, high-value validation today (Acknowledge **effort** or **intent**, not just the result).	**Empathy Check (Chapter 5):** When reacting to a colleague, quickly ask: "What non-hostile **Contextual Stressor** might be driving their behavior?"

The Crisis Sequence: When Conflict Hits

Use this structured sequence to move from an emotional outburst (hostility) to a constructive solution (integrity).

Phase	Action Tool	Goal
1. Stop the Burn (Book 2)	**4-7-8 Breathing Protocol:** Inhale 4, Hold 7, Exhale 8 (repeat 4 times).	**Restore PFC Function.** Stop the physiological surge and calm the amygdala.
2. Check the Story (Book 2 / 1)	**Reality Testing:** Isolate the factual observation from the **Hostile Attribution Bias** Generate 3 non-hostile alternative explanations for the behavior.	**Prevent Rumination.** Force the mind out of the toxic replay loop and into objective data.
3. Assert the Limit (Book 3 / 5)	**DESC Boundary Script:** Define the limit clearly and assertively. D (Describe fact) → E (Express need) → S (Specify rule) → C (Consequence: *Your* action).	**Uphold Integrity.** Defend your boundary with conviction.

| **4. Problem-Solve (Book 2)** | **5-Step Model:** Use the controlled calm to initiate structured problem-solving (Step 1: Define the factual problem). | **Find a Solution.** Address the root cause of the conflict, replacing helplessness with competence. |
| **5. Repair the Rift (Book 3 / 5)** | **Accountable Apology:** If you contributed to the damage, apologize by naming the specific behavior and the **violated need** (e.g., need for respect), followed by a clear commitment to future action. | **Rebuild Trust.** Close the accountability gap and reinforce the relational bond. |

HERE'S ANOTHER BOOK BY VIVIAN WHITMORE THAT YOU MIGHT LIKE

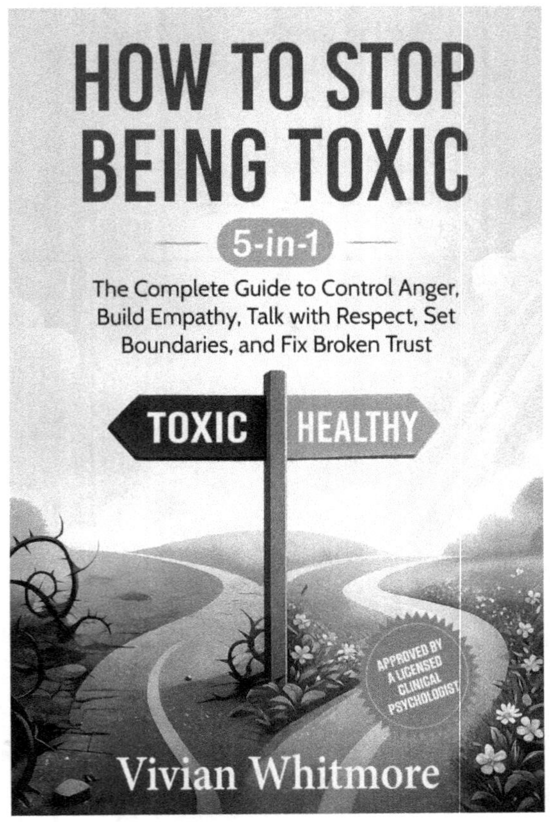

Claim Your Free Bonus

As a thank you for reading, I've put together a powerful digital bonus pack to help you apply what you've learned — even if you only have a few minutes a day.

 **Inside you'll find:**

- ✓ Quick-access emotional reset tools
- ✓ A printable clarity map for focus and purpose
- ✓ 30 powerful journaling prompts
- ✓ Daily progress & reflection trackers
- ✓ A mini affirmation deck for calm and confidence

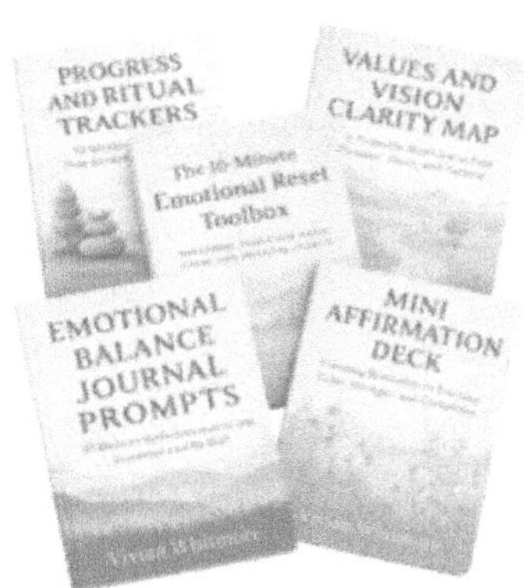

Access below to download your full bonus pack:

https://livetolearn.lpages.co/vivian-withmore-how-to-stop-being-negative-rude-and-hurtful-5-in-1-paperback/

Or, scan the QR code

COMPREHENSIVE RESOURCE INDEX

Book 1: Rewire Your Brain: Action Steps to Boost Positivity

Introduction

https://pmc.ncbi.nlm.nih.gov/articles/PMC3652533/

https://pmc.ncbi.nlm.nih.gov/articles/PMC7047599/

Chapter 1

https://fortmyerstherapist.com/cbt-technique-using-triple-column-technique-change-thoughts-change-life/

Chapter 2

https://pmc.ncbi.nlm.nih.gov/articles/PMC8475916/

https://pmc.ncbi.nlm.nih.gov/articles/PMC10440210/

Chapter 3

https://rickhanson.com/online-courses/positive-neuroplasticity-training/

https://rickhanson.com/topics-for-personal-growth/the-negativity-bias/

Chapter 4

https://medium.com/@msjag416/dopamine-and-learned-helplessness-why-motivation-disappears-and-how-it-comes-back-39853a4f49a7

https://www.chapterstreatment.com/post/taking-action-a-guide-to-action-oriented-therapy

Chapter 5

https://www.kevinwgrant.com/blog/item/breaking-free-from-self-judgment

Conclusion

https://digitalcommons.pcom.edu/cgi/viewcontent.cgi?article=1024&context=capstone_projects

Book 2: Take Back Control: Techniques to Calm Anger Now

Introduction

https://www.centerwatch.com/clinical-trials/listings/NCT06697587/enhanced-cognitive-reappraisal-and-emotion-awareness-training-ecreat-for-maladaptive-anger-inhibition-a-pilot-study

https://pmc.ncbi.nlm.nih.gov/articles/PMC3490066/

Chapter 1

https://www.psychologytoday.com/us/blog/the-athletes-way/201905/longer-exhalations-are-an-easy-way-to-hack-your-vagus-nerve

https://www.healthline.com/health/4-7-8-breathing

Chapter 2

https://pmc.ncbi.nlm.nih.gov/articles/PMC4849278/

https://pmc.ncbi.nlm.nih.gov/articles/PMC12452349/

Chapter 3

https://pmc.ncbi.nlm.nih.gov/articles/PMC3490066/

https://cogbtherapy.com/cbt-blog/2014/5/4/hhy104os08dekc537dlw7nvopzyi44

Chapter 4

https://pmc.ncbi.nlm.nih.gov/articles/PMC10243415/

https://pmc.ncbi.nlm.nih.gov/articles/PMC4176893/

Chapter 5

https://pubmed.ncbi.nlm.nih.gov/26592092/

https://www.neuroregulation.org/article/view/23500

Conclusion

https://mindful.health/anger-management-techniques/

Book 3: Connect Clearly: Actionable Models for Kind Speech

Introduction

https://www.verywellmind.com/being-direct-vs-being-rude-8739387

https://www.verywellmind.com/what-is-prosocial-behavior-2795479

Chapter 1

https://www.theoaktreepractice.com/resources/relationships/how-nonviolent-communication-can-transform-your-relationship/

https://www.hatching-dragons.com/blog/nonviolent-communication-principles-practice-benefits

Chapter 2

https://www.mayoclinic.org/healthy-lifestyle/stress-management/in-depth/assertive/art-20044644 https://www.mdpi.com/2071-1050/13/20/11504

Chapter 3

https://pmc.ncbi.nlm.nih.gov/articles/PMC2717040/

https://pmc.ncbi.nlm.nih.gov/articles/PMC3021497/

Chapter 4

https://pubmed.ncbi.nlm.nih.gov/34963634/

https://www.kevinwgrant.com/blog/item/breaking-free-from-self-judgment

Chapter 5

https://www.natibeltran.com/the-complete-guide-to-nonviolent-communication-for-purpose-driven-leaders/

https://www.hatching-dragons.com/blog/nonviolent-communication-principles-practice-benefits

Book 4: Build Inner Strength: Daily Habits for Practicing Gratitude

Introduction

https://www.scielo.br/j/eins/a/m8kqK5vgZ9wb4DxRtD877bd

Chapter 1

https://www.piedmont.org/living-real-change/the-life-changing-effects-of-gratitude

Chapter 2

https://positivepsychology.com/neuroscience-of-gratitude/

Chapter 3

https://www.cannelevate.com.au/article/gratitude-letters-research-written-appreciation-wellbeing/

Chapter 4

https://positivepsychology.com/neuroscience-of-gratitude/

Chapter 5

https://www.mindful.org/the-science-of-gratitude/

Conclusion

https://www.scielo.br/j/eins/a/m8kqK5vgZ9wb4DxRtD877bd

Book 5: Define Your Space: Practical Actions to Spread Respect

Introduction

https://www.ebsco.com/research-starters/social-sciences-and-humanities/social-exchange-theory

Chapter 1

https://health.ucdavis.edu/blog/cultivating-health/how-to-set-boundaries-and-why-it-matters-for-your-mental-health/2024/03

Chapter 2

https://www.mayoclinic.org/healthy-lifestyle/stress-management/in-depth/assertive/art-20044644

https://www.ahrq.gov/teamstepps-program/curriculum/mutual/tools/desc.html

Chapter 3

https://en.wikipedia.org/wiki/Social_exchange_theory

Chapter 4

https://www.verywellmind.com/what-is-prosocial-behavior-2795479

https://pmc.ncbi.nlm.nih.gov/articles/PMC3490066/

Chapter 5

https://www.therapyroute.com/article/100-therapy-questions-for-self-awareness-healing-and-growth-by-therapyroute

Conclusion

https://cogbtherapy.com/cbt-blog/2014/5/4/hhy104os08dekc537dlw7nvopzyi44

https://www.mayoclinic.org/healthy-lifestyle/stress-management/in-depth/assertive/art-20044644